FOR THE *Love* OF A CAT

A Publisher's Story

DAVID ST JOHN THOMAS

FOR THE *Love* OF A CAT

A Publisher's Story

DAVID ST JOHN THOMAS

EXISLE
PUBLISHING

First published 2006
This edition published 2009

Exisle Publishing Limited
'Moonrising', Narone Creek Road, Wollombi, NSW 2325, Australia
P.O. Box 60–490, Titirangi, Auckland 0642, New Zealand
www.exislepublishing.com

National Library of Australia Cataloguing-in-Publication Data:

St John Thomas, David

For the love of a cat : a publisher's story / David St John Thomas.

ISBN 9781921497360 (pbk.)

Includes index.
Bibliography.

St John Thomas, David.
Publishers and publishing—Great Britain—Biography.
Cat owners—Great Britain—Biography.
Cats—Anecdotes.

070.5092

Designed by Christabella Designs
Typeset in 11pt Sabon CE Roman
Printed in China through Colorcraft Limited, Hong Kong

10 9 8 7 6 5 4 3 2 1

To the memory of Sara

What greater gift than the love of a cat?

CHARLES DICKENS

CONTENTS

PREFACE

'But there are so many cat books already; can you possibly find something to say?'

A typical comment from non-cat lovers who heard I was writing this. They have a point, for there are more copies of books about cats than cats themselves in most English-speaking countries.

The reaction of cat lovers among my friends was predictably enthusiastic. When was the book going to be ready? Would I make sure to tell them when it was published? And, 'I can't wait.' One cat lover placed an order for six copies even before the title was decided.

Populations can be divided in many ways: golfers and those who haven't got the bug, for example, or those addicted to surfing the Internet and those who can't stand computers. Nothing, however, is more decisive than the difference between cat lovers and the rest.

These words are unashamedly addressed to those who love cats, who may already have all the cat books they 'need' on their shelves, but hopefully will enjoy a different angle and being introduced to my personal range of cat personalities. The answer to why I have written it is that I have something to say. I hope you enjoy it.

David St John Thomas

Chapter 1

THE SOUL OF A HOME

The door was answered by a harassed woman who asked me to step inside quickly as she was on the phone. Pushed into her drawing room, to my delight I was followed by two Siamese chocolate-point cats still in the flush of youth. I spoke to them, made a high-pitched sound and licked my lips. By the time the woman, a well-known literary agent, had finished her complicated argument with another publisher, they had competed for the best place on my lap. The loser had flung its front paws up on my chest and was looking longingly into my eyes.

'How did you manage that?' asked the agent accusingly. 'They don't like people. They're a mistake. Apart from screaming for food, they ignore me, and the more visitors try to make a fuss of them, the less they want to know. They're weird – and you must be, too, attracting them like that. But then I've never understood you or your kind of books.'

I was a successful international book publisher, the 'David' of David & Charles in Devon, England, and over the years, my love of books and cats had become connected. The business side of the conversation has long been forgotten but, not surprisingly, my company never published a book from that agent. The cats were, however, a bright interlude in a busy day spent dashing around London over a quarter of a century ago, and ever since I've wondered what became of them and whether they ended up with the better owner they deserved. They will have died years ago. Maybe I am the only person who remembers them fondly.

The literary agent had probably acquired them to enhance the décor of her cream-and-pale-chocolate drawing room, and a pretty addition they made. Her understanding of them was zilch; that they so rapidly appreciated my love showed how desperately they needed it. How pleasurable it would have been to take them – their loud, steady purrs and penetrating blue eyes – home with me ... except that my own chocolate-point Siamese, Sara, who would purr for me when I reached home in Devon late that evening, would surely have seen me as a traitor destroying her world. Sara was my cat ... and I belonged to her.

The only thing that could be said for the literary agent was that, although she was unable to give cats the appreciation they deserved, at least her pair were company for each other. She certainly would not have understood that, desperate for human company though they might have been, like most cats they had to be in control and make the first move. As with any self-respecting feline, they would naturally have walked away from those who overpoweringly chased them and prematurely yanked them onto their lap.

'If ever I have a cat book looking for a home, I'll think of you,' was the agent's parting shot, probably the sole indication she ever gave of my being worthy to handle a publishable manuscript that came her way. I have no memory of why I went to see her, and even with the temptation of the two Siamese, I had no reason to call again. If she is still alive, it is a safe bet that she won't be with replacement cats today. Unless someone else with a publishing background unfortunately recognises her and points these remarks out, they will not offend her since a cat book is highly unlikely to interest her.

It is not only those who are unworthy to own cats who may lack an understanding of their elementary psychology. Cats are wild creatures yet have great sophistication, the powerful Ferrari of small animals who, since they were treasured in ancient Egypt (even accidentally killing one carried the death penalty), have been tamed and bred to live with us. But we need to appreciate the constitution of their bodies and souls. All cats share a set of deep, basic instincts more universally than do dogs.

A cat is always a cat, a self-serving hedonist, excelling at simultaneously being independent and making humans serve its needs. Yet, as the only wild animals to choose to do so, many cats also excel at being an important member of the family, and love their favoured human so dearly that they go to great lengths to cherish him or her, showing real friendship – friendship way beyond looking after their own needs and certainly having nothing to do with food. That is a recurring topic in these pages.

P. G. Wodehouse said, 'Cats, as a class, have never completely got over the snootiness caused by the fact that in Ancient Egypt they were worshipped as gods.' Such is their independence that no cat is permanently on duty at the beck and call of its owner. But then how many humans are instantly available when their cat wants their attention? In the fascinating relationship between the different species, there are often periods of intense enjoyment alternating with those of going different ways, of plain ignoring each other even when only feet apart.

The better we accept that, the more matter-of-fact we can be in our understanding of it, the richer will be the enjoyment of our cats. 'Time spent with a cat is never wasted,' said Colette, to which Jean Cocteau added, 'I love cats because I enjoy my home; and little by little they become its visible soul.'

Millions of people, including many authors, painters, musicians and politicians of the less dictatorial kind, have found that having a cat is a vital ingredient in turning a house into a home. In later pages we will see examples of how this works. Here let it suffice to say that it is from the army of cat haters that many cat lovers are recruited – often because a cat simply walks into their lives.

Writing this book has given me much pleasure, largely because it has helped me to increase my knowledge and further enhance my love of the species. I have been introduced to dozens of cats and told of many extraordinary happenings. One thing especially stands out: the large numbers of cats who walk into a new home. At least one in ten of the cat owners with whom I have spoken insisted they had no intention of acquiring a cat but that one had acquired them. Two I have recently been told about are Poppy and Nipper, who have moved into different homes miles apart.

Typically, Poppy 'just arrived', a malnourished kitten of about ten weeks. With cat logic, because her face was coloured like a winter pansy she was called Poppy. 'Well you can't shout Pansy outside your house, can you?' said the owner. Pretty Poppy instantly settled in, toileting and so on without problem. This was where she belonged. A few days later she was taken for a check-up at the vet's, in a cardboard box because there hadn't been time to buy a cage. 'There's commotion and commotion,' said the owner. 'You never heard the like of it. She virtually ripped the box to pieces. She was absolutely frantic.'

She obviously feared she was going to be dumped for a second time for, when carried by the owner into the surgery, she calmed down and behaved with dignity; and on the way home, her owner comforting her with sweet nothings, she was content to know she was returning with the one she was going to love, to the place she had chosen to live. Being dumped, especially in a sack, must be a truly frightening experience.

Nipper's tale is quite different. He also just turned up and was given what was intended to be a very temporary home since he matched the description of a cat that worryingly had been reported missing from a local animal shelter. Nipper instantly settled in – far too well for the liking of his temporary carers who had sworn they would never have a cat. So what happened next? The local paper arrived, prominently featuring the return of the real lost kitten to the animal shelter's tender care. A victory not only for Nipper but for the species, for now the owners couldn't possibly be without a cat.

All over the world cats are constantly converting people. I doubt any political or religious movement regularly makes so many converts. Naturally many former cat haters continue to rail at the species; it is just their individual pet they enthusiastically 'tolerate' because it is 'quite different'. Of course, eventually there will happily be a 'unique' replacement.

Never have there been so many lovers of individuals of anything that they are so much against as a group. No wonder the advertisements of charities offering kittens and cats for re-homing write creative notices and advertisements describing very individual animals. All intended to persuade someone to do what they have always said they wouldn't: have their home brought to life by a cat.

There's no emptier place than a dwelling without animals; cats add life to our own lives in so many ways, says the UK's main cat charity, Cats Protection. And the Australian Animal Protection Society says of Charcoal, its latest 'Cat of the Week':

> *People tend to walk right past Charcoal's pen. They think she is too old and not worth meeting. It almost makes us cry to watch. People have no idea what they are missing. Charcoal is so gentle and has the most gorgeous placid nature. She is considered middle aged (she is eight years old) and is so very special to us because of her beautiful, settled aura. Charcoal is pure gold.*

No doubt many people's defences are weakened by tales of the conversions of others and by the cat-lobby's spontaneous witness. Just before reaching this point I took forty winks, then opened the latest issue of the *National Geographic* magazine where, in the correspondence column, I found this short testimony by Laurie-Anne Gauvreau of St-Omer, Quebec, Canada:

Cats can help the mentally ill by providing unconditional love and giving them a sense of responsibility. Cats can be beneficial to our health, as simply stroking them can relieve stress and lessen the pain of a headache, and they provide companionship for the elderly. As we live longer, there is greater demand for that companionship.

The UK's Cats Protection says that 15 per cent of the cats it re-homes go to those over 65; while in a survey half the cat owners aged over 50 said that having a cat made them feel younger. Later we will discuss how cats themselves are also living longer.

Another reason why people are converted to cats is the extraordinarily successful public relations cats somehow achieve. Many commercial public relations firms, charging millions, would surely be delighted by the positive news coverage and the column inches devoted to them. A variety of examples are cited later.

Included in this public relations coup are details of famous cat lovers, past and present. American Presidents, British Prime Ministers (Winston Churchill, hero of World War II, even had one sit in on cabinet meetings while another, Margate, slept with him after he turned up as a stray on the doorstep of 10 Downing Street), and other top people from all kinds of fields, especially authors, were or still are real enthusiasts. Again examples drift across the later pages as I tell my personal cat story, which hopefully will make its own new converts. Just one more comment here: in the darkest days of the war, when Britain's prize *Ark Royal* was sunk off Gibraltar, morale didn't quite take the expected plunge because, in addition to the rescue of all but one of the crew, people took comfort in the fact that the two ships' cats, Oscar and Harry, were safe. As with much to do with cats, it might not be rational, but it is true.

So back to our starting point: there is a simple explanation behind the commonly expressed statement that cats pursue those who dislike them rather than those longing for their company. Exuberant but unsophisticated cat lovers approach them too rapidly, assuming rather than earning trust and interest. Those who prematurely plonk them on their lap find they jump off and are reluctant to return. The cat haters who remain aloof seem safer to approach. This feline quirk is not the cussedness it is taken for.

Which brings me to the first rule of cats: always let the cat make the first move. You can open a conversation with them, smile at them, and offer them your hand at a safe distance. Only attempt physical contact when they have initiated it, usually by sniffing your outstretched finger or rubbing against your leg. It is of course hard to teach this elementary rule to children, whose physical size might be less frightening than that of an over-bold adult, but who often destroy the possibility of confidence by shrieking or laughing and moving rapidly.

Rule number two is never to laugh at a cat or let it think you are ridiculing it. You can talk to a cat. Only if you build a close relationship, can you occasionally laugh *with* one. Never *at*.

In the following pages, among the many cats we meet will be those from my parents' home and – much later – the cats that have very much belonged to me. The first of the latter was Sara, to whose memory this book is respectfully dedicated. That we were to have a Siamese was decided after much discussion and argument between myself, wife, daughter and son. I am not sure if Sir Compton Mackenzie's warning deterred or egged us on: 'People who belong to Siamese cats must make up their minds to do a good deal of waiting on them.'

One momentous day, we all went to fetch *our* kitten. We had a whole litter to choose from. The owner, in a private house, not a cattery, offered to hand us the one she thought would be most suitable. 'No,' I said. 'Let's see if one of them comes to me.'

I knelt down with outstretched hand and addressed the half dozen kittens and their mother. Several came for cursory inspection and returned to the family fold. Then one of the smaller ones with a piece of inferior string for a tail, which she somehow managed to keep erect, and who unsuccessfully attempted a meow, strode up and nudged my middle finger. She responded to my delighted reaction and danced around me. She purred and I recalled that someone had once quoted an ancient saying: 'Never underestimate the power of a purr.'

It was the start of a 21-year love affair, which has inspired both this book and a continued affection for the species that has helped keep my health and spirits in trim. She was Sara: Sara the unforgettable.

Chapter 2

MAKING FRIENDS

Those who have read this far will be familiar with the scene. A respectable-looking chap walking purposefully suddenly stops or, if there is another human being around, lingers until he is on his own. He has spotted a cat, maybe in a nearby hedge, or outside a front door, or even across the street.

He squeaks to it, remembering the cat's range of hearing is more highly pitched than our own. The cat meows, and a conversation is established. In some cases the cat positively rushes, jumping up on a wall, or rolling at the man's feet. It might even dash across the road, care of course having been taken to ensure it is encouraged only when there is no traffic. In other cases it is harder to make contact, and progress is slow and furtive. The cat needs pauses to build up confidence, while one of those inevitable urgent itches is dealt with or a smell taken in. It might stop a few feet short, but is always allowed to make the final approach, even if it rolls, exposing its tummy, a couple of feet away.

Usually the conversation leads to stroking – and purring. A shy cat might only make one dash to sniff the proffered finger and then retreat to a safe distance. The most wary, while not achieving even a sniff, still show interest and will patiently continue meowing, perhaps exposing their tummy at a safe distance, clearly enjoying the contact. Urgency and patience, as appropriate, are two leading cat characteristics. Probably both, but certainly patience, come from the hunting instinct.

After a few moments, and often because another human approaches, our chap resumes his walk and the cat returns to the spot where first seen. Both feel uplifted, happier for the experience. The man's blood pressure has probably dropped.

My choice of gender is deliberate for usually such scenes involve a stooping male. Possibly more women than men are cat lovers, but women are more conscious of what people think of them, probably less willing to be seen in what neighbours might regard as a foolish light. It is, however, only in our time, in the second half of the lives of older people, that it has become acceptable for men to show affection for cats. Even today I might be viewed as an oddball conversing with a cat a fraction of my size; until well after World War II there would have been a danger of being seen as mad or perhaps an unfulfilled pansy.

Prior to this, though many people, especially the elderly living alone, had become heavily reliant on the friendship of their pet, and even some farmers secretly petted their favourites, cats weren't seen as warranting special attention. In pre-1939 days, few country vets paid much attention to them. When training, James Herriot couldn't find a decent textbook on them; the vets' bible, the huge Sisson's *Anatomy of the Domestic Animals*, didn't even have cats in the index. It was indeed Herriot's books and TV's *All Creatures Great and Small* that encouraged wider interest in the unique behaviour of cats.

Of either sex, the skilful cat attracter knows the essential rules. By all means take an encouraging lead, letting the cat know you admire it and have only the friendliest of intentions. Converse with it as an equal. When it is only a few feet away, encourage it by smiling and show your tongue by licking your lips. Never make the final approach. Cats have to be in control. If you lack the time to allow the cat to weigh you up a dozen times over, move on rather than frighten it. You might possibly still have started a relationship to build on if you pass that way regularly.

Rolling on the back, exposing the tummy, usually says the cat also has friendly intentions. Once it has sniffed your hand, rubbed itself against your legs, or you have stroked its back, especially just in front of its tail (which shoots up in appreciation), you are accepted. Yet not always totally, for some cats, even if they then roll and seem to invite your stroking their tummy, see it as taking too great a liberty if you actually do so. But then many cats show trust in their owners by exposing their anal region.

The wildness in some cats – often those abused when young or not taught social skills in those first formative weeks – is never far from the surface, and a sharp claw travelling at the speed of greased lightning easily draws blood. Don't blame the cat. Retreating to a safe distance, it might still enjoy your company, and you its, perhaps while happily chasing the end of a long stick. Your blood pressure might still come down.

Naturalists tell us that there has to be an advantage for both sides in encounters between creatures of different species. The need for friendship even in the cat who usually prefers to walk alone is as strong as it was for a donkey and a large brown trout who became inseparable friends, until the trout was claimed by a fisherman and the donkey's distress knew no bounds. (This remarkable behaviour was observed by the English naturalist W. H. Hudson.) The most social of humans frequently suffer from a very basic loneliness. Constantly in company, we feel we have to keep up our end in what amounts to a continuous round of public relations. Exchange a few moments of companionship with a cat on your walk, and there are no social, business or other compunctions. All the cat requires is interest and respect.

You can talk to it in gibberish providing it sounds sincere. You might well conclude that you'd have every reason to worry if your son or daughter behaved like the cat. But a cat is a very different creature who has been bred to enjoy our company while retaining infinitely more independence than a dog or the family pony. Forget all about human values and aspirations. The cat we meet in the street isn't seeing us a source of food, only as a transient passer-by. If another friend, especially a child comes along, the affection might instantly be transferred. To the true cat lover, that should be a source of pleasure, not jealousy.

Mind you, occasionally a cat falls in love with an appreciative passer-by. A Devon woman carrying heavy shopping bags was followed street by street until she reached home. The cat wouldn't be shooed away, but hastily slipped through the open door. It wasn't interested in what was in the bags; it liked the lady, and knew a good owner when it saw one. Years later it still lives with her, taking mere incidental interest in the arrival of new shopping but ever ready to welcome her back home. In another Devon village, a cat fell for the parson. It followed him to church daily until it actually moved into the church. Unfortunately, its messing up the altar cloth resulted in a prohibition order.

Most of the best encounters tend to be matter-of-fact affairs. The cat and the human enjoy a few moments of shared affection and are the better for it. What else can so effectively raise one's spirits? Is it surprising that hotels with a welcoming cat seem to exude greater warmth, or that the more enlightened old people's homes encourage visits by those prepared to lend their cats for an hour or two's social duty? A cat, or an aquarium, can be counted on more reliably to reduce tension than a visit by a friend or a spouse weighed down by the troubles of the world – difficult journeys, getting parked, deciding when bills should be paid or just finding a vase for new flowers. Yet we also are animals, more sophisticated and weighed down by pressures maybe, but still with basic, earthy instincts.

There are many reports of the therapeutic value of cats in old people's homes. For example, an old man at a seniors' nursing home in America only came down from his room on the day a cat visited. Then, though normally he only reluctantly spoke in a whisper, when asked if he'd like the cat on his lap, he almost shouted 'yes'. He stroked it as though it was the greatest achievement of his life – which it probably was.

Children don't care if they look ridiculous, are generally less pushed for time, and somehow have greater confidence that their overtures will be welcomed. Patience, however, is naturally sometimes short. One says 'naturally', though isn't impatience encouraged by the competitiveness of the world? The child most insistent on having the latest fashion in trainers is probably also the most impatient to conquer a cat, perhaps frightening it by lurching at it.

Happily many children are quick to learn that the cat has to make the first move – and a gentle child must seem altogether less threatening than a towering man swinging his arms. Even two year olds can learn that lunging at a cat is less rewarding than giving it a gentle stroke.

Child–cat friendships can be spoilt by the child being more patronised by adults than is the cat. We are all creatures deserving of being treated sensibly. My sister Ruth has never forgotten that she was treated well below her intelligence and emotional capacity when our parents decided the time had come to put Sam down without attempting to explain why his ailment made it unkind to keep him longer. I was 'trusted' to break the news, with devastating effect – especially as Sam, of whom more later, had been brought to our Devon home in Teignmouth by Ruth after he had been found wondering homeless at a Girl Guide camp on Dartmoor.

Once, if one of several cats living together died, it was thought best to 'disappear' it quietly. Now it is acknowledged that it is kinder to show the body to the other cats and let them realise what has happened. If I go before my beloved Skye, I hope she might adjust more easily to my loss by seeing my body than wondering why I simply walked out of her life.

That I was lonely as a boy (my only close school friend died suddenly) might have something to do with why I seemed naturally to like cats and make friends with them. Fortunately, perhaps, I didn't come in contact with them until I had some understanding. What a catastrophe it is when confidence is destroyed by a baby so delighted at the first sight of a mammal that he or she laughs aloud. Cats have long memories and being ridiculed is unforgivable, even from a baby hanging out of a pram and giggling with sheer delight at the tail on four legs below.

My early cat memories are vague about timing and places yet crystal clear about each cat and its individuality. The roadside encounter with a ginger tom whose tail shot up every time I made gentle conversation with it; the purr of a tortoiseshell who chose to jump onto my lap at a children's party, having instantly jumped off the laps of two children on which it had been placed by a manipulative grown-up. The first time a cat rolled for me was outside a hotel in Hythe in Kent on England's south coast. My elation was followed by horror, a feeling that the bottom had fallen out of my world — could there ever again be enjoyment in being on holiday? — as the cat caught sight of a mouse and showed off, tossing it, letting it recover and tossing it again. How could something be so gorgeous yet so cruel? The sooner one learns about all aspects of the cat's behaviour, no doubt the easier it becomes to accept the seamier side.

It was Sam with whom I first forged a deep friendship. But let us explore what we mean by friendship. Friendship goes well beyond behavioural patterns, including play that practises hunting, for the survival of the species. W. H. Hudson says that the 'union or feeling of preference and attachment of an individual towards another of its own or a different species' is ...

> *unconcerned with the satisfaction of bodily wants and the business of self-preservation and the continuance of the race. It is a manifestation of something higher in the mind,*

which shows that the lower animals are not wholly immersed in the struggle for existence, that they are capable in a small way, as we are in a large way, of escaping from and rising above it ...

Friendship is in fact the highest point to which the animal's mind can rise. For whereas play, which has its origin in the purely physical state of well-being and in instinctive impulses universal among sentient beings, does indirectly serve a purpose in the animal's life, friendship can serve no useful purpose whatever and is the isolated act of an individual which clearly shows a perception on his part of the differences in the character of other individuals, and also the will and power to choose from among them the one [with] which he finds himself most in harmony.

Real friendship cannot be selfish but does require response. In cats, that means occasionally behaving in a manner that goes beyond the usual 'I'll do what I want'. Respect or love may be greater on one side or the other, but friendship implies delight in doing something that overcomes convenience, greed or laziness. The cat crying for food will forget its hunger when its owner, the one it loves, returns home.

The human must be understanding. My Siamese Sara, my steady companion for 21 years, found it as hard as most of her species to awake from a snooze beside the fire, get to her feet and jump onto a lap. Cats bear no malice, so the thing to do was to throw any convenient lightweight object such as a newspaper at her to rouse her. She then unfailingly — eventually — jumped onto me, licked me gently on the tip of my nose and cradled herself in exactly her regular position in my arms for a long, deep purr. If I had not understood her desires and total matter-of-factness about being woken up, some bedtimes would have passed without showing our love for each other. Only occasionally, when I was in her bad books, did we go our separate ways for the night without reassuring each other of our mutual friendship.

Friendship is beyond affection. And preference sorts out especial friends. Except in the case of one-person households, the one who provides the food (and who will be followed around and harassed until it is provided) is frequently not the special friend. Feeding is a necessity; friendship is a choice. Rivals and even enemies respect the need for food and often declare a truce at feeding time. Certainly there is seldom hostility among cats at feeding time, though most gobble favourite food as though still in the days of wartime scarcity. An older cat I knew who spent hours hissing and generally being unwelcoming to a young visiting stray had just begun her dinner when she broke off to fetch the impostor. They shared the meal in peace. Hostilities soon broke out again. This pattern was repeated for several days. Whether the pair might eventually have settled down together we won't know for the older cat died from eating something poisoned it found on its rounds. The youngster took over the territory, bed and feeding bowl, though behaving very differently in most ways.

The instinct to help, especially with food, is strong – and, of course, not only with cats. A flock of migrating birds will wait while a sick one is fed, and a blackbird has been known to feed a thrush with a broken beak.

Naturally, the demarcation between instinct and friendship is sometimes hard to discern. Some of those extraordinary journeys cats make home when they have accidentally been driven away in a car or lorry, or wandered too far, are obviously heavily instinct based. Some journeys, scores or hundreds of miles across country, back to old homes underline the point that the physical home is more important to many cats than the occupants. However, some cats, especially of Oriental breeds, forge human bonds far deeper than the security offered by a familiar building. Some left at their old home on purpose, or accidentally, somehow navigate dozens of miles to return to the family fold. Reunion with humans, occasionally after years, brings obvious joy, demonstrating deep personal friendship. How curious is the balance between instinct and choice.

Though most readers might not realise it, that is what makes newspaper reports of cats surviving against great odds and returning home after long absences so popular. I was still a boy when I started enjoying such stories and noticed that cats appeared in the headlines far more frequently than dogs, or probably all other pets together.

The theme is nearly always their independence versus their need for human support, their hunting instinct versus their cheerful generosity. 'Happy ending for Malaysian stowaway' introduces us to a ginger tom who arrived emaciated and dehydrated but eager for life after three weeks in a shipping container. Note how, even in newspapers largely filled with stories of disasters, 'happy' and 'cat' are frequently tied together. 'Story ensures cat's tale has happy ending' describes how a French family moving to Scotland were reunited with their long-haired black Roquette who had gone walkabouts in the Borders. A photograph of the stray published in an earlier edition happened to be seen at a real estate agent's a friend visited, setting the process in motion. My examples mainly come from the UK but when I have been in Australia, America and elsewhere in the English-speaking world I have noticed that cat stories are given wide prominence. Howie, a Persian, crossed the rivers, deserts and wilderness of the Australian outback to reunite himself with his owners when they moved to a new home a thousand miles away.

Tom the tenacious seems to hold the record. It took him two years to travel the 2,500 miles from St Petersburg in Florida to San Gabriel in California to achieve his happy ending.

There was another happy ending for Chloe who, when only five weeks old, made a 133-mile journey across Scotland under the bonnet of a stranger's car; a rescue centre gave her love and attention and she went to live with a student nurse who had spent the summer as a volunteer there. Meg, a 'right little madam' with beautiful blue eyes and a pathetic little squeak, also hitched a lift and was spotted jumping out of the car and into a vent in a cathedral wall; she got stuck in an organ pipe for several days. Told that she refused to come out, her owner came along and was overjoyed when she instantly responded to her voice. You can almost hear her complaining: 'What kept you?' Sometimes of course newspapers assume their readers like to read half-solved riddles. For example, why was Scooby found 145 miles away from the home where his owner had died? Such stories usually inspire several people to respond with information or offers of a new home.

In Bude, North Cornwall, even a cat's own burial ended happily – at least for that cat and its owner – when it leisurely wandered into the garden as a deep hole was being dug for it. The look-alike dead cat belonged to a neighbour. Often it is not known why a cat disappears, where it has been and how it comes back. White short-haired Snowie, who vanished for eighteen months and then returned to take up its old routine as though nothing had happened, belonged to the daughter of our local bookseller, George Gray, in Nairn, Scotland, where I now live. 'Cats are quite astonishing,' he commented. 'Such a mixture of qualities topped by a zest for life.' So at least one bookshop will give this title prominence.

If you stop to think about it, perhaps one of we humans' nicest traits is that we want our cats to be happy. We are given loads of advice on how to ensure they have long and healthy lives, a favourite instruction of mine accompanying a pet cushion being: 'First remove pet, then wash at 40 degrees.' There are books and numerous magazine articles with advice on how to have a 'Happy Cat' or 'Contented Cat'. And an endearing characteristic of cats is their determination to make the best of things. That's their instinct, we might conclude; but there is also choice in it. For example, they love teasing us — disappearing into the undergrowth and ignoring instruction to come this instant, only to surprise us when we least expect it. Great fun.

Deciding to jump on us to be caressed is a positive choice. Seeking such delight goes miles beyond instinct. And what is at work when a timid cat who hates being picked up becomes ill and surrenders itself to its owner, purring gently as TLC begins to take effect? Many are the stories of cats who first bonded closely with their owners as the result of having to be cared for. Some cats who are ill may wander off secretly to die, but most will sacrifice their independence to regain health. Is their joie de vivre in fact just instinct? For that matter, is it human instinct to go to such trouble to ensure our cats are happy? Obviously not, for in past times most cats were left to fare for themselves. Perhaps we are all getting soft? Yet what greater joy do we experience than when seeing our cat in rapturous contentment, or even when giving a few minutes of pleasure to a cat we stop to pet in the street?

Instinct or choice: the topic is bound to reappear in later pages.

Often it is the cat following a basic instinct that opens up the possibility of developing a special relationship. For example, when a long-haired tabby was found huddled against a doorstep of a semi-detached house on the edge of Bath, he was seeking survival: food and shelter. No cat was welcome in that doggie household but, with that persistence that cat haters see as cussedness, he wouldn't be sent away. At breakfast on the fourth day, he was still there huddled up in a tight ball – waiting patiently. This was to be his home!

By the time the owner came back from a day's work late that afternoon, which happened to be Friday, the heavens had opened. The cat, small enough even with long fur, was now an insignificant soaked ball. 'Oh well,' she said. 'You'd better come in.' Tail up, he instantly did. He walked confidently around the house and up the stairs, inspecting each room before returning to the kitchen through which he had arrived. The cat was firmly established by the time the owner went to work on Monday. That evening she thought she should take him to the vet for a check-up.

'What's it called?' was answered by an instantly decided 'Jimmy'.

'Jimmy, LH tabby,' said the vet, writing it down. Questioned how he knew the cat was left-handed, the vet replied, 'Long-haired!' and then inspected a scar on a hip where the LH had been shaved off for an operation; the vet couldn't imagine what, but Jimmy (estimated to be two and a half years old) had obviously been cared for. It was the start of the summer holidays. Had the owners simply tossed him out of a car on their way to the seaside?

Jimmy developed into quite a character; for example, taking a complicated and very indirect route from the ground to the top window of the first floor bedroom via a shed, garage and another window ledge before his final jump. He sometimes landed on the bed gently to pat open the eyelids of the occupants if he thought they were sleeping too late. Unfortunately his memory went awry at 3am one morning and he landed on the bed of the cat-hating neighbours, who phoned demanding his immediate removal and punishment. It was all too clear to Jimmy he wasn't wanted there.

He tolerated dogs providing they didn't interfere. When a huge German shepherd began raiding his food, blood spluttered out of the dog's nose swiped by a claw. Thereafter the dog gave Jimmy a wide berth, a supertanker going out of its way to avoid passing close to a yacht.

The point of this story is that while Jimmy respected the owner and brushed against her appreciatively when, for example, she was preparing his food, theirs was a pretty matter-of-fact relationship. It was her husband, who did very little for his physical welfare, whom Jimmy came to adore, spending long evenings on the back of an easy chair looking as though he were on the man's shoulder, though maintaining eye contact. He purred gazing into his eyes.

Little is straightforward with cats. One day an owner relishes a Siamese's friendship, the next he will be snubbed. One afternoon the cat lover working in the garden will have a friend never more than a few feet away, following her from job to job. Next afternoon, not only is there neither sight nor sound of yesterday's faithful companion but, when the cat does return home, the merest glance at its stance signals independence — 'Leave me alone.' Yet hours later it will follow her round the house to demonstrate she's a lifelong friend, and the next day will become deeply involved in the gardening by moving the planting line so it is no longer straight, or imitating its owner by digging little holes for the plants.

There is an ultimate test. If a human friend is in trouble, the real cat friend seems to know and play its part, sometimes uniquely relieving the pain of parting with another member of the human family through death or desertion.

While I was writing this I had an operation. Skye, one of my current Balinese cats, and the subject of a later chapter, somehow knew. Unexplainable but true. She yowled and yowled in a quite unfamiliar way just when the operation was taking place. Nothing would console her. She's often reported as unhappy when I'm away, but this was different. A few days later, when I returned home with bandage, she wouldn't take her adoring deep-blue eyes off me. There are many such recorded incidents. For example, a woman reader from Penzance in Cornwall wrote to *Your Cat* magazine about Lily, normally 'very much Daddy's girl' who suddenly wouldn't be kept off her lap when she suffered a sudden pain down her side. 'She was most persistent, pressing her face into my right side and making the most peculiar noises she never made before and I've never heard since ... I'll always feel Lily was trying to help me take away the pain.'

The extraordinary sensory perception of cats in knowing if their owners are in trouble or dead is frequently commented on. Though they cannot bark or howl like dogs, they find plenty of other sounds and signs to show their concern or grief ... with psychic timing. When hope was given up for the owner of Mopps and Smartie and he was dying at home, they slept continuously on his bed, one remaining on duty during the short periods the other had to do essentials elsewhere.

On the death of their owners, cats behave in very different but unusual ways; for example, staying on their owner's favourite chair (or studiously avoiding it), guarding the door to their room, or expressing special concern for the surviving spouse. My daughter's Burmese, Tulip, said farewell in sombre mood to my grandson Mathew by spending the entire funeral service, conducted at home, sitting on his head as he lay in his coffin. In Lincolnshire, an owner told how Thomasina used to sit on her husband's knees, which she did for longer periods until his death. On the evening of the funeral, she said her farewell by jumping onto the cardboard box containing the urn with the ashes, which had been left on top of a chest of drawers. She spent the whole night purring on it 'as if she was saying goodbye'. Though usually a sign of contentment, purring is also said to be restorative and it might well have been her way of coping.

These and many other examples surely demonstrate friendship; nay, love. Though Orientals are known to show especially strong feelings, they are well outnumbered by ordinary moggies displaying extraordinary friendship or love.

The more we understand about cats, perhaps the more we still have to learn. It is easy to realise how their mystical qualities frightened suspicious people in the past. Cats were naturally associated with witches, and pure black ones were once so exhaustively slaughtered that to this day in Britain we scarcely see one without at least a few white hairs.

Conversely, for generations black cats have generally been associated with good luck, but they are not everyone's favourite and a disproportionate number land up in cat shelters. At the time of writing, the UK's Cats Protection is running a special campaign to persuade people to 'adopt their very own lucky charm'. Among famous people who really believed in the black cat's good luck was England's King Charles I. His pet (or symbol) was carefully guarded day and night. Ironically, it died the very day before he was arrested, a key moment in his battle with Parliament that led to the Civil War and Charles I losing his head.

While it has to be admitted that many cats are control freaks, it is their uncanny ability to understand what is going on (a subject to which I will return) that upsets many humans who believe our species has the exclusive right to be in charge and in the know. For many, the dislike, verging on fear, goes with the assertion that 'cats only do what they want'.

'They're stupid. They sleep all day, and want our attention just as we're going to bed and it's too late' sums it up, though usually it is an even less subtle 'I gave you your chance, but you wouldn't come. Now I'm busy so push off.' Okay, we humans are unique with our brainpower enabling us to conquer the world, even if routinely we partly destroy bits of it. But does that give us the automatic right to determine exactly at what time we're free for our cat(s) and when we are 'engaged'?

True cat lovers are those who have learnt this is not the case, and who respect the cat's right to be a cat. Even with another human, harmonious living involves compromise, and with a cat, if we think about it, we can manipulate a constructive meeting of ways. For example, if our cat is sleeping later than usual and is in danger of missing the evening cuddle, by all means wake it just in time. As already said, whatever else their faults, cats don't bear grudges. Providing it's not deep into their sleeping time, they quickly forget it is you who woke them and turn on the engine of their purr, cuddler and cuddlee in harmony. But we cannot expect them to be totally at our beck and call.

Certainly I have learnt to enjoy their company beside me as I write. My cats relax me and cause far less interruption to thought than even the simplest phone call about what time dinner will be. They sense when the writing is going well and seem concerned when it isn't. 'Why don't you marry a cat?' I was once asked by someone who thought I was obsessed. That misses the point. The relationship is special because it is across species. This was something appreciated by Charles Dickens, the novelist, who doted on his cat at a time when most Britons took them very much for granted – much as today we do mice. He summed it up perfectly when he said, 'What greater gift than the love of a cat?'

Chapter 3

EARLY LEARNING

Few of us can remember when cats first made an impact on us. 'I've always loved cats' alternates with 'I don't really remember'. The moment of conversion is rarely recalled or passed down by elders. Those brought up with taken-for-granted cats might naturally have assumed them to be a routine but unexciting part of life. Even if we remember a cat first coming to live with us, few of us felt its arrival was a life-changing event. In most families the installing of the first radio or TV caused more stir. Most parents who felt it was the thing to do to have a cat were matter of fact about it.

A few recollections of encounters with cats before our family owned one (or rather, one owned us) have already been cited. During the war, when we were evacuated from Teignmouth in South Devon to South Molton in North Devon (1942–44) we had a cat with an extra front claw, but memories are stronger of the neighbour's white Persian vigorously rejecting overtures and nearly scratching my eye while hissing at me. Persians, especially white ones, are among the few cats I have never taken to in later life. They have strong devotees, but at cat shows I pass them by since there are too many cats of other shapes and sizes more clamorous in their need for attention.

Much to my surprise, I later discovered that the white Persian who hissed at me was blind. Since he seemed to lead a normal life and was an efficient mice-killing machine, it made me realise just how different cats are, with extraordinarily well-developed feeling, sense and hearing systems. Cats could forecast storms and even the danger of air raids before the warning sirens, we were told. They certainly knew the difference between the warning warble and the welcome one-note all clear. In fact, one of the first things cats taught me was how totally different their senses are from ours. Through their patient observation, they surprise us by knowing more than we expect; for example, cottoning on to the fact that a visitor is deaf and tapping their legs as they never normally do to attract attention.

After we had returned to our own home near the end of the war, there was that memorable day my sister brought Sam home. We cannot now remember if he already had that name or we bestowed it on him. Sometimes he was called Sammy but plain Sam suited him better. A handsome outgoing cat, he quickly made sure he was the centre of the family's focus, but it took time for him to win my love, and for him especially to befriend me. Dad hadn't wanted a cat, and my first thought was being grateful to my sister for 'bringing it off'. Mother pronounced that an animal would be 'good' for us and undoubtedly a cat was seen as better than rabbits and less demanding than a dog. A dog was anyway out of the question, for the house had to be kept quiet for Dad's work as author, poet and literary journalist.

How many millions have 'had' a cat primarily because of the advantage that it doesn't bark or need taking on walks? Sam was too much of an individual properly to conform to these favoured negative traits. He liked walks. Whenever we set off, there he'd be following us, meowing, asking if we would slow down a bit to let him catch up. Often we climbed to the top of our steep road to catch the bus into town. Sam got to know our return time and met us, running ahead, tail periodically erect, as we carried the shopping home down the hill. Dad particularly hated him accompanying him on his morning walk, which he preferred to do alone 'to touch his muse'. And even at home Sam insisted on being heard as well as seen — heard here, there, on the wrong side of a door, wanting food or a game.

Dad, it soon became clear, was anything but a cat lover. He couldn't bear Sam, or any other cat, on his lap or rubbing against his leg. Feline verbalising was anathema. Sam, Dad learnt, could most easily be shut up by being fed. All he had to do was scream and brush against Dad to be given food — instantly. Mealtimes multiplied and became steadily earlier, Sam steadily heavier. 'How else can I have peace in my own home?' Dad asked plaintively. The rest of the family protested that he had become a slave to Sam's appetite and was doing neither himself nor the cat any good.

It was at that point I learnt that in families cats usually become emotionally closer to those who don't feed them than those who do. I virtually never fed Sam, but steadily we seemed to explore each other's souls. He was the first of many cats who have enjoyed lying on me upside down. He would land and wriggle almost simultaneously so that all four paws were in the air, and break into a deep purr the moment I acknowledged his uniqueness in the universe.

The first books I bought myself were in Dent's King's Treasury series, a kind of poor man's Everyman's Library.

Under the general editorship of Sir Arthur Quiller-Couch, at less than 6 pence in today's money, cheaply but soundly produced jacketless hardbacks just under 6 inches high by just over 4 inches wide, they opened up new horizons. Lamb's *Essays of Elia*, Shakespeare's plays and the natural history writings of W. H. Hudson were among the many treasures readily available in pre-war editions published primarily though not exclusively for the educational market.

There were two reasons that delayed my natural progression to the more adult and larger Everyman's Library, famously expanded in breadth and depth by its poorly paid editor, Ernest Rhys. One was that they were harder to obtain in the shortages of post-war Britain – once the manager of the local WHSmith criticised me for buying new volumes too rapidly after they were put out on rather bare shelves. The other reason was that they were too heavy for Sam to have balanced on his four raised paws. He was delighted to serve as book rest for the King's Treasuries, though wasn't particularly keen on my turning pages to look up references or answer the questions most volumes set for young people reading them. Perhaps it was Sam's fault that I developed an almost irrational dislike of being quizzed about a book I had just read. So often the questions seemed to depend on remembering trivial details as opposed to absorbing deeper messages.

While most cats regard reading as an unwarranted diversion from unadulterated admiration – they have a great ability to sit exactly on the part of a double-page spread we are reading – Sam happily accepted the triple relationship between him, me and the book to whose enjoyment he contributed. He realised he'd spend longer in his favourite position, his purring occasionally quickened by a recital of sweet nothings, if he served as a book rest. Usually I stroked him while turning the page, so he looked forward to my completing another double-page spread, providing I didn't keep turning pages to consult the exercises.

It was while Sam was acting as book rest that, in his *Birds of Wing and Other Wild Things*, published in 1930, I suddenly came across Hudson devoting a few pages to cats, especially London ones. He said that, so far as he knew, not a word had previously been written on them, introducing a theme that crops up occasionally later in these pages. Cats were things you just had, not of sufficient interest to make other than a casual appearance setting a scene in a novel, certainly not to be seriously discussed or to become involved with emotionally. We'll return to Hudson's comments anon.

Apart from their ability to survive, cats have two great characteristics: to insinuate themselves and take over, whether they are wanted or not, and to adapt and learn. Sam was master of both. When Dad walked round the garden, Sam knew his route and jumped out to surprise him at various points. While hardly anyone came in our house without being conquered in a friendly way, and Sam was an absolute essential of family life, he seems to have concluded that Dad was an inferior kind of human, good for being fed by but lacking in understanding. He teased, if not tormented, rather than loved him. It was an intelligent cat's way of constructively making the best of a bad job. While many famous authors have enjoyed a cat sitting peacefully at their side while composing in silence, and have celebrated their special cats in poetry and prose, Dad's study was out of bounds. Enjoying other ways of being the centre of Dad's attention, wisely Sam didn't even try to slip into it. How delighted I'd have been had Dad loosened up and furtively welcomed him on his roll-top desk.

Another peculiarity is that cat lovers are often less concerned about their pet's welfare or temporary disappearance than those who profess not to care. If Sam ran up a tree, somehow Dad knew instantly and complained his concentration had been spoilt. Suggestions to let him find his own way down were brushed aside. Send for the fire brigade! They came on several occasions, frightening Sam who climbed higher to be out of harm's way and hung on more precariously than before. Sensibly, the fire service no longer routinely turns out to rescue cats. Try your local animal shelter for advice. Avoid shouting and certainly throwing things. Once they are no longer the centre of attention, most cats safely make their way down even if it is dark. Hunger is a great stimulant.

Sam was a remarkable creature, establishing for me a lifelong love of grey cats. He delighted in planning ahead, and perhaps has been the cat who came closest to laughing. He was wonderfully adept at increasing the repertoire of games with a ping-pong ball on linoleum. His right paw sent the ball accurately back a score or more times to whoever was playing with him. He'd cover up our mistaken shots by instantly bringing the ball back to its proper course, moving briskly almost before one had misaimed; indeed he could tell what kind of shot we would make before we made it. Then he'd have his fun, suddenly darting off here and there, ready for the ball to ricochet at high speed into his paw, until – with obvious satisfaction – he aimed it back at us perhaps just before we were about to give up. He, not we, would determine when it was time to drop the game. All the rules were his. Yet there was a proper team spirit.

Then things went pear shaped. It was alleged that Sam had a serious health problem and he was collected by the vet to be put down. I remember little of the detail though have always thought that Sam might have lived a decent further life. There was too much matter-of-factness, too little emotion, in the decision. In later years I came to see the loss of our family cats in much the same class as Mother's restless gardening desires, prematurely out with the old and in with the new, in reaction to which I developed a pathological hatred of throwing plants away and struggle to keep them alive well past their usefulness. In any event, my parents asked me to break the news to my sister that Sammy was no more, with the devastating result mentioned in the previous chapter.

I lost my first real friend. I still see Sam's grey and white paws stretched from his white undercarriage propping up those King's Treasuries. The power of human recall is a curious thing; while many practical, everyday details have been forgotten, if I open up some particular volumes, the very thoughts experienced reading with Sam's purr in the background come back in the same way that listening to a piece of music can remind you of what was happening when you first heard it. With Sam, schoolwork revision was more relaxed and memorable. If only I had been allowed him on my lap in the exam hall.

Our next, and last, family cat was a quite different proposition. Lulu liked her comforts and needed human company, but was much more self-contained. Maybe fearing she wouldn't last long, I hesitated from investing too much in building a close relationship, but she probably wasn't that kind of cat anyway. A well-groomed tortoiseshell, she was handsome and knew it. She was an observer rather than a doer. She wouldn't dream of following one along the road, but spent hours in a crotch of a tree overhanging our gate, in whose brick post was a letter box. People posting letters, the postman emptying the box four times a day (in those days a letter collected at 2pm caught the town's 4pm delivery), visitors and tradespeople all paid their respects, which she accepted with dignity rather than warmth. In a haughty kind of way, she enjoyed a joke at other people's expense. Among the naughty things we children did was use a long piece of string to hold the gate open and release it to crash with a bang, disturbing old ladies posting a letter. With a smirk akin to that of Alice in Wonderland's Cheshire cat, Lulu looked down but never acknowledged anyone pointing her out as though she were the culprit.

Dad, of course, didn't like her jumping onto his lap, and fed her prematurely to pacify her. He wasn't however prepared for her getting in the family way. Her courtship was riotous, with local toms fighting each other while she looked on. She fell for what seemed the least desirable of a ragbag bunch, a fierce fighter who arrived bedraggled and, after frequent copulation, was rudely chased away by a satiated Lulu. Naturally, they had to do their lovemaking outside my window disturbing the little piece of garden I tended. Nothing would dislodge them from the flowers trodden-down by them.

'That's nature for you,' said Dad, widening the gulf between humans and the lower realm of pets, 'they're driven by instinct and selfishness.' Which gave him another occasion to tell the story of how a poor woman who had recently moved had taken her unhappy cat to the People's Dispensary for Sick Animals, where the pronouncement was that it was sulking. Naturally. But the distraught owner wasn't content, and foolishly (Dad implied) had taken it to a private vet. The verdict? It was 'pining'. That's what you got for spending your money: blindfold sympathy for the cat who couldn't cope with a simple move.

Lulu being pregnant was surely going to give trouble. Where did she choose to have the babies? In one of the drawers of Dad's desk, among the assortment of chocolates he had kept for another occasion, loose among tobacco that had fallen out of packets stored there. Ye gods. The very devil couldn't have created more disturbance. The desk, by the way, could be accessed via a gap at its rear, for the backs of the drawers were not as high as their fronts. Earlier the chewing up by mice of corners of manuscript left in the desk had been blamed on Lulu. 'If you haven't got them already, a cat will give you mice' was part of quoted wisdom along with 'Everyone knows that a female cat will not be healthy if not allowed to have one litter of kittens'.

Though probably enjoying the commotion she created, and totally lacking Sam's fear of visiting the study, Lulu came to realise that bringing up a family in such alien territory wasn't ideal. One by one she carried the newly born kittens down the cellar steps and hid them well out of reach on a patch of sloping earth under the lounge. She probably wasn't a bad mum, but oh the anxiety she gave us, especially we children. Pleas to keep at least one of the kittens fell on deaf ears. There was even talk of having the gardener drown any who couldn't be found good homes. All were quickly reserved before they were weaned, delivery being delayed until the first indications of their different characters came out.

Of Lulu's end I have but the dimmest of memories. I cannot be sure if she was put down or given a new home. What I do recall is Dad's relief when the house was cat free and that it was extremely unlikely there would ever be another challenge to his authority.

In Dad's defence, he wasn't unique in not being able to understand the simplest cat psychology. Nor does the fact that no dictator has ever liked cats mean that he was one. The tragedy lay in the rest of the household being unable to make the most of our cat because he couldn't hide his unease. The slightest overture by Sam or Lulu had him in a tizz. Cats, surely, were to be seen, not heard.

Sam and Lulu wound him round their little tails, food provided as soon as they demanded it. If they didn't like exactly what was put before them, it was proof that they were spoilt – 'Suppose we were that fussy?' – which of course missed the whole point. Cats are not substitute humans but a very different species. Imagine Lulu in human terms as your girlfriend or daughter and you would blanch with good reason. But a cat is a cat, and we shouldn't expect it to think and react as we do any more than we are surprised it cannot recite its alphabet. Alas, Dad always saw differences as deficiencies. 'They rely more on smell than sight,' was once said accusingly. For a writer who had 'to get on', even Lulu's patient waiting for an opportunity to claim his chair was anathema. Thieving was unwarranted, not natural.

If my wife gets excited about our Balinese getting into the dining room and having a feast as well as a romp, tipping out the contents of the sideboard, she agrees that it was her fault for not locking the door from the kitchen. It is not fair if one day we enjoy them pushing open the loo door to see how we are doing, and are fascinated by complex manoeuvres to open the linen cupboard, and the next blame them for tackling the meat left out to thaw. Foolishly, Dad believed cats know right from wrong. They do quickly cotton on to what is *allowed* and what isn't – without being able to understand why. This adds zest to exploring their cupboard of goodies when it is not bolted and we're not there to shoo them away. What spoilsports we must seem.

While I knew Dad was wrong in judging things in human terms, it set me thinking. A moment of revelation was when we shouted at a cat for bringing in a mouse. The message received was probably of disappointment that we had only been offered so small a one ... or perhaps had hoped for several. Much though I hated seeing cats torment mice – how joyful I was when a mouse standing tall on its back legs used its front paw to give its aggressor such a bash on the nose that, in a moment of confusion on the cat's part, the mouse escaped down a hole – I came to realise the inevitable: the hunting instinct is so powerful that it determines much behaviour.

The patient waiting for an opportunity to take over Dad's chair was intrinsic since you don't catch mice without a lot of hanging about. When Lulu walked slowly crouched as though she were invisible, she probably thought she was, unobserved by her 'prey'. Games with ping-pong balls or screwed-up pieces of paper are of course hunting related. Every cat I have seen, including our own, naturally resorts to the deception of allowing the plaything to think it has been forgotten – and so is safe – only cunningly to attack it afresh from some new angle. What kitten can resist a rapidly moving object such as a pen doubling up as a mouse?

I came to learn that increased tension while waiting to be fed – not that Dad kept our cats waiting – was caused by inherited anxiety as to whether the next kill would be successful. I once visited a house where the moggie relieved the tension of waiting for food by making her tail soaking wet; her owner said that when she was hunting she sucked it if a mouse didn't present itself soon enough. (And remember that roughly only one in three final pounces on a patiently stalked mouse succeeds.) The fridge replaces the mousehole to wait by. And so on. Nothing we humans can do will eradicate this nature-given hunting-based behaviour. Even the cat's hearing and ability to feel the minute vibrations of a mouse and to use its whiskers (which is why many blind cats are prolific hunters) emphasises its design as a killing machine, a miniature version of the lion or tiger and other big hunters.

Yet many cats truly love their owners and are cuddly animals, needing us, and frequently at the centre of family life. It is our luck that, unlike the lion or tiger, even in anger or accident they are not large or powerful enough to cause humans much injury. Is it surprising we are so fascinated by them and that here is yet another book about them? People who are especially harassed sometimes say that in their next incarnation they'd choose to be a cat with everything provided for, little anxiety and plenty of leisure. As the essence of the cat came into focus for me, I became less sure. While cats may be good at making the best of things, the lottery of their lives is too great. Inevitably cat lovers get to know best those who, as we say, have fallen on their feet. Not all enjoy a life of Riley; and while material things such as warmth and medical care have improved, loneliness as owners stay out longer at work and suburban boredom aren't to be envied. I decided it was nicer being a human with cats.

One of the first books I read about cats was *A Cat Affair* by Derek Tangye, whom I used to meet occasionally donkey's years ago. Derek's tales had considerable vogue in their day. He had left MI5 literally to carve the meadows round his Cliffside cottage to create the fields for his Cornish flower farm. The back-to-nature angle went well with his insight into the cats of successive generations that insinuated themselves into his precarious lifestyle. He was one of the first authors to get into a cat's mind, to make one feel what it was like to be rejected or accepted, deprived or given comfort — and appreciate the fight they'd wage for a place in the family home. 'It was a maddening situation. Deep down inside me I remained anti-cat,' pleads the author. 'And yet I had to admit to myself that my anti-cat defences broke down whenever an individual cat chose to entice me with its charms.' Sound familiar?

In the works of Derek Tangye, there are unpredictable episodes in the long drawn-out fight, but guess who wins in the end? In *A Cat in the Window*, he shows real understanding.

Now that the three of us were always together, Monty was spoilt. But is not a cat's nature, any cat, impervious to being spoilt? You can spoil a child and it can become a nuisance. You can spoil a dog and everyone except its owner is certain to suffer. A cat on the other hand, however luscious may be the bribes, remains cool and collected. Indulgence never goes to its head. It observes flattery instead of accepting it. Monty did not consider himself an inferior member of the household; a pet, in fact. Thus he loathed it when condescension was shown to him; and many a misguided stranger trying to lure him with snapping fingers and 'pussy talk' has seen his haughty back. He was co-tenant of the cottage. He was not to be treated in that imbecile fashion so many people reserve for animals.

If only more cat owners understood that — most of this book is in a sense an attempt at a very similar message — how much happier owners and their cats would be. At least I never started by being anti-cat myself, though possibly Derek Tangye had the advantage of the passionate zeal of the newly converted.

Chapter 4

CATS AND PEOPLE

At least Dad was honest, making no pretence of liking cats. Reluctantly, a cat had been acquired because it was the thing to do for the benefit of the rest of the family. Less to be respected are those who buy a kitten at Christmas without any long-term commitment or provision in mind; and, perhaps worse, those who have a cat or cats as personal effects or as part of the décor rather than to cherish, the literary agent mentioned in Chapter 1 being a sad example.

This is being written with my current pair, brother and sister Arran and Skye, sleeping beside my desk. The point of mentioning them now is to say that possibly one in eight people who come into my study show clear unease. A small proportion have a physical allergy. A few of these much regret the need to have 'such lovely things' removed or – in extreme cases – to ask if we could meet in another room since, even if they have been removed, the air will remain contaminated. The remainder simply dislike (or fear) cats. Most in this category just about tolerate them while no doubt thinking I'm pretty weird having them alongside me while I write. A few – and to my mind *they* are the weird ones – grimace and say they cannot stand cats near them.

They might attack or, worse, ingratiate themselves. 'Will you protect me?' asked one woman. 'I couldn't stand them jumping on me.' Or 'I can't bear to touch a cat or have them rubbing themselves against my legs.'

Someone who does occasional ironing agreed to come only on the condition the cats were kept out of her way: 'Arran might jump on me.' That has a happy ending, because one afternoon she shared the kitchen with a cat lover who refused to shut them out. 'I think Arran likes me,' said the ironing lady when I popped in. Next visit: 'He definitely likes me.' The one after that: 'He jumped up on me, bless his heart.' Now the worry is that he won't do so. Soon after, a stray white cat decided to make his home with her; now Frosty is all in all to her. Arran has changed her life.

If humans would only relax, cats are wonderful conquerors; but then a refusal to be melted is the very reason some humans are so icily stand-offish. That is particularly sad with young people. I knew a couple of girls whom it might have been easier to persuade to do almost anything than allow an animal to express friendly intent. 'Thank you, I don't want cat hairs on my skirt.'

Nature might not have intended it that way but, after thousands of years being part of our households, the role of most cats is to make people more relaxed and therefore better. Many cats certainly know it. If only at their convenience, their friendship brings joy. Their love greatly enhances the lives of many people, especially those living or spending long hours alone.

Yet, sadly, even many who love cats bring the worst out of them. As a youngster I undoubtedly treated cats and kittens too boisterously, encouraging rough play with consequent scratching. When Arran arrived and, as a three-month-old kitten, occasionally drew blood on our hands and fingers, I taught him the word 'Gentle'. Say 'Gentle' and he will immediately withdraw his claws and expect to be stroked. Yet when I tell visitors playing with him on their lap to say 'Gentle', they respond by saying any other word: 'Stop it.' 'That's not nice.' 'Be careful.' 'Don't be naughty.' And so on. 'No,' I say. 'He only knows Gentle and No.' So what do they do? Go on saying anything else. It is beneath their dignity to adopt the limited language cats know. Is it surprising there is not better understanding?

Apart from a few very specific words, it doesn't matter what you say so much as the tone of voice you say it in. Skye soaks up sheer gibberish as loving praise but, even though we belong to each other, I have to be careful not to ridicule her. Try saying that to many people and the response is usually high-pitched laughter of course taken as ridicule. Cats are far more sensitive of mood than humans – and don't always get the humans they deserve, which is why many skilfully re-home themselves.

It is especially distressing for older people when things go wrong. Because some lonely people's dependence on a cat knows no bounds, their pets are often spoilt – or worse. Perhaps the first time I fully realised this was when a specialist bookseller in Leamington Spa, who had been giving good business to my rapidly expanding publishing company and with whom I had established a friendly relationship, finally explained why she couldn't come out to lunch. A middle-aged spinster, she had obviously appreciated being asked, which is why on successive visits I had repeated the invitation. After a string of 'I'll consult the diary and let you know if I'm free', I'd come to know her well enough to be told the truth.

'Pleasant though it would be coming out with you and talking about our favourite books, unfortunately I've a prior commitment every day. Percy my cat gets upset enough if I keep him waiting on the doorstep because I'm a few minutes late. He'd never forgive me if I didn't come back for lunch at all. I have to fit my life around him.' Percy was as vital as any husband. Yet who is to say that is wrong, let alone tragic?

Where do we draw the line? Later I was to come across several authors who couldn't come to visit the office, or to meet me in London, or anywhere really, because their cats couldn't be left. No, they couldn't go on TV to be interviewed about their new book, sign copies in a bookshop ... anything. The cats were in control or, in some cases it seemed, out of control with total possessiveness.

Yet even in the heat of the moment, upset at having lost valuable publicity, I wondered if I was right to be critical of my authors. Having become highly dependent on the animal for company and purpose in life, it is hard to let it down. In a couple of cases, one of a pair of cats had died. They had been bought to give each other company, and the remaining one, now in its old age, had become ultra dependent on the human. I suppose it depends what we want in life. Skye and Arran won't keep me off TV, yet I know they deserve quality time and I am happy to give it to them.

One author didn't mind leaving his tortoiseshell girl and grey boy by themselves, since whenever he arrived home they were asleep and seemingly self-content. Yet one day the person living opposite said how pleased he must be to find the cats so eagerly waiting for him. 'They're looking out the window at least an hour before you're expected.' The little devils had apparently waited until they saw or heard him, and then dashed to bed to feign sleep and total indifference. Once the truth was out, the owner was so flattered that he spent more hours at home and was less willing to visit the office. Another feline victory.

Surely true friendship demands give and take, at least a touch of equality. And, like children, cats need to know the limits. Silly indeed is the human who becomes too dependent on a cat only to allow it to turn into a bullying control freak who has learned exactly how to get its way. Many cats undoubtedly domesticate (and dominate) their humans.

Cats becoming too possessive tend to be of two main kinds. First is the timid cat who was poorly socialised in its early days. Owners frequently pick pets to match their own disposition, and a timid cat over-protected by a cautious owner results in the latter becoming a full-time minder who is punished if they fail to deliver what has come to be expected. I know of several owners who have totally cut themselves off since their cats don't like visitors or being left alone.

Second is the sensitive yet confident cat (often a pedigree) who is matched by an obliging owner so anxious to be supportive that they destroy any hope of real partnership or friendship. Such cats cannot play second fiddle and often turn to unsocial and even downright unsavoury behaviour and bullying. A bachelor Glasgow publisher once had such a Siamese. Though no doubt lovable on its own terms, it couldn't tolerate not being the centre of attention and, among other problems, totally wrecked his home. Examples abound of this kind of cat knocking things down and causing damage to get their own way. If they want the door opened they pretend they need to pee only instantly to wail or scratch to be let back in. An extraordinary range of tactics can be displayed to make their mere human offer their lap or even give up their favourite chair by the fire. In such cases the cat's weapon is its patient persistence. Humans are their mice.

Another way in which cats win is to devise chasing games in which the humans play their preferred role. Often these begin with the cat chasing after a ball the human sends spinning. Craftily the rules then change so that the cat takes things more easily and the humans do the running around. One couple I knew were encouraged to throw a piece of screwed-up paper to each other while the tabby, Jock, tried to intercept it as it spun over him. If he intercepted it, he would chase it around. Eventually, however, he lazily lay on his back and only batted the 'mouse'. The fun now was seeing the humans crawl around doing the chasing. A case of 'cat in the middle' instead of pig.

From time to time many of us naturally complain about our cats – as we grumble about our husbands, wives, children and the telephone or TV. While we may never exactly win over our cats, and are wise not to expect to do so, at least we maintain a 'dialogue' and enforce some kind of discipline, often happy to spoil them but knowing when to say no.

Flattery is potent. In our cut-throat world, being really appreciated has become rare, especially for people on their own and retired couples who find it hard to relate to outsiders and shy at joining a club or social organisation. A cat's (or dog's) love is the greatest appreciation many humans enjoy. Is it surprising they soak it up irrationally? Fortunate are those of us who can enjoy a cat's love in perspective, as an extra ingredient of life's rich tapestry. But who am I to speak of perspective? Skye has just interrupted me. By various tactics such as rolling on this manuscript, talking and repeatedly trying to get me to follow her to an office chair on castors, she has just made me take her for a ride. What am I doing pushing a cat around the office when I should be writing?

The desire to control, by human or cat, is perhaps a freak aspect of love. It afflicts extreme cat lovers – people who can never have too many felines. Most of them are women, their homes totally devoted to cats who sleep on all the beds and eat from rows of individual dishes supplied from burgeoning larders. Especially when they die, and a dozen or more cats have to be found new homes, such people often get into the news but are seldom understood. Many of them look vague. Their lives are based on an unsolvable dichotomy. They are control freaks carrying heavy responsibilities involving long hours and hard physical work which curtails their freedom. Yet cats can never be truly controlled since in nature they are lone creatures. The more of them competing for love and attention, the less fulfilling individual relationships can be.

Other such people, 'real animal lovers', have hoards of horses, donkeys, pigs and other livestock. 'Too busy,' they cry if invited out. Many so committed to cats and other animals are short of money since their responsibilities deny time even for casual work and animals are not cheap to feed and keep healthy. Some who no doubt started as cat lovers became totally overwhelmed by their menageries, which disintegrate into filth until the animal inspectorate is brought in. It is forgotten that cats never naturally socialise en masse and, deprived of individual human attention, those from such places are hard sensibly to re-home.

Another astonishing aspect of cats is the huge amount of money spent on them. Guess who pays for the lavish budgets devoted to advertising rival brands of cat food? Cat beds and carrying cages become steadily more elaborate. Cat psychologists (or behaviourists) thrive. On duty at a New York cat show, giving relaxation therapy to an Abyssinian kitten, one behaviourist said she charged $100 for a telephone consultation and $200 for a house visit in Manhattan. Now, in Britain, you can invest £62 in a Cat Toilet-Training System so that your cat can share the toilet seat with you. A cat-controlled lever to flush will no doubt be next, if it hasn't already been invented in Japan.

Then, not knowing what else to give them, relatives of cat freaks send furry toys, cat cards and themed presents (such as cat statues) for the owner. There are many fine statues, bronzes, glass cats and so on. If you are waiting for God, having downsized into sheltered accommodation where no pets are allowed, maybe cat substitutes play a role. We have one in our catless wee holiday home. But if you have the real thing, why pack mantelpieces and windowsills with inanimate felines? Real cats are, well, so much more real.

Many cat cards are artistic and truly catlike. While I am not enamoured by cats writing phoney messages to each other, it is hard to throw away cards with an evocative picture outside and a tale about a friend's cat and its latest prank inside. My collection steadily increases. But there is only one cat picture on the wall — a painting by a cat-loving artist who was writing a book and happened to visit on a day when I was low with the grief of having lost my own cat. It arrived with a note 'to cheer you up', and has hung by the study light switch ever since, an amazingly life-like portrait of the artist's own grey cat, his dignified head speckled with thin white lines and his cheek lit up by pale threads pointing to a fine crop of short, white whiskers, giving me pleasure long after the artist and his cat have disappeared from the scene. Incidentally, have you noticed how frequently grey cats with benign expressions feature on greeting cards? My last birthday brought one with his tongue out. I've been wondering why ever since.

Statues and other imitation cats also serve a role for those who cannot bear the thought of a moggie bringing in thrushes and sparrows yet feel it cruel to keep a pet indoors. What tangles of argument cats cause us to have with ourselves. While Britain's traditional special relationship with the United States might currently be under strain for political reasons, consider how much harder it would be to establish transatlantic harmony if it depended on reconciling views on giving cats their freedom outside or keeping them wholly indoors, and letting them retain their claws as nature intended or removing the front ones for safety.

In Britain, even if you have a decent cat run and live in a largish house, you still feel it necessary to explain why your cats are indoor ones and occasionally feel guilty that they are deprived from their natural roving and hunting. In the States, where many more live in apartments, not only is it unavoidably necessary to restrict the freedom of cats in a larger proportion of homes, but even in country districts many believe it is cruel to risk allowing cats their freedom. Declawing, unacceptable in Britain, has become the norm in much of the States. Arguments for and against are seldom discussed rationally. 'Catty' more accurately describes the lack of tolerance cat lovers with opposing views have for each other than anything to do with the character of cats themselves. Cat spats are short-lived, for whatever the situation, most cats find a modus vivendi. Not so their owners discussing the rival philosophies of caring for them. Australians, however, are more laid-back, especially on the declawing issue.

Just how strongly people can feel about animals was first brought home to me when, as a teenager, I was persuaded by the district organiser to do a house-to-house collection for the Royal National Society for the Prevention of Cruelty to Children. At least a quarter of those who answered their front door made it clear they would have been more generous had I been collecting for animals. One or two said that they more or less believed in cruelty to children, for there were too many of them and those who survived would mainly have a sticky end anyway. Such was the gloom of the early years of the Cold War. Dogs and cats, according to individual preference, could do nothing but good. Only my kneeling on the front door step to talk to their cat persuaded one couple to give something to children. (Many door-to-door salesmen trade on ingratiating themselves to a cat or dog.) Then there was the elderly lady who said she needed to save every last penny so she could leave a worthwhile sum to her cats when she died.

It was when later I published a book whose royalties were donated to the Cats' Protection League (now just Cats Protection) that I realised what large sums *are* left to animals. My contact was the treasurer, who a decade earlier had been an assistant at Hambros Bank. My fast-growing publishing company had been brought up short by the sudden financial crisis of 1974–75, and Hambros were giving me a bad time. This unusually gentle banker said nothing when his colleagues even threatened me with personal bankruptcy. He stayed while the others went off to discuss my fate. 'Remember,' he said, 'they might take your money, but they can't take away what you stand for and what you care about.'

Out of the blue, he then asked if I liked cats, and when I nodded, added that he had assumed so. 'Now, when they come back and say what they're going to do, don't let your whole being be at stake. Think of a cat.' At which point the bosses returned.

A dozen years on, *A Passion for Cats* sold well, especially through the WHSmith chain. At the end of the first year's sales, I sent a royalty cheque for £37,000 to Cats Protection. Not bad, I thought, wondering how it might be spent to benefit the cats.

Next morning the treasurer was on the phone. 'Congratulations,' he said, 'and don't be put down by what I'm about to tell you. Indeed, in future we might benefit from more of what I'm about to tell you as the direct result of the book. But in the same post as your letter we received notification of one legacy for £1 million, and another for £4 million. Quite embarrassing really.' And when you think what £5 million in the 1980s might have achieved in improving water supplies in darkest Africa, embarrassing seemed the word. Which naturally isn't to say that much of the work of Cats Protection isn't vital and gives good value. Or even that every apparently extreme cat lover necessarily has a warped value system.

There are fanatics in most walks of life, and none more so than in the cat world. Fanatics who raise large sums of money, who skimp and save to leave more in their will, and fanatics who are less well equipped to deal with human beings than their cats.

In Melbourne, Australia, a couple offered a unique prize, a Porsche, to anyone finding their five-year-old Burmese, Rusty. The owners reasoned that, sleeping, eating and watching TV with them, he was worth more than the luxury car. They could get another car. There was only one Rusty. Who among readers of this book who have lost a cat could say that was fanatical? Alas, the car was never claimed; Rusty had clean disappeared, leaving the owners as bereaved as though a child had been kidnapped.

We can never see one of those frequent 'Cat Lost' notices or advertisements without sparing a thought for a grieving owner. And I always give a special thought to pet lovers who have moved into a flat or apartment and have been allowed to bring an existing pet with them but never to replace it. What agony its death must cause. If you might be planning to end your days in such a flat, try to do so with a youngish pet.

So where do we draw the line between normal people in the middle of the extremes of those who cannot stand the sight of a cat and those who devote their total lives to them? Normality, remember, doesn't mean being totally rational. While cats, or dogs, or for that matter donkeys or homing pigeons, cannot be the be all and end all of balanced people leading fulfilled lives, cats in particular bring out extraordinary reactions. No wonder film stars see them as too competitively 'sexy' to appear with them. Yet millions of us would find our lives seriously emptier without our very special cat or cats. Invariably and inevitably they have more in common with other cats than dogs of different breeds do with each other, yet are such splendidly quirky individuals. Over history they have made their special mark with writers and publishers and other creative types, but they conquer all manner of people. And not least among them is the person who never intended to share their life with a cat but finds it has gained new purpose when one selects their home to move into.

James Herriot, perhaps the author I as a publisher most regret having rejected, describes a Mr Fawcett after the death of his wife.

> *He lived alone on his old age pension. It wasn't much of a life. He was a quiet, kindly man who didn't go out much and seemed to have few friends, but he had Frisk. The little cat had walked in on him six years ago and had transformed his life, bringing a boisterous, happy presence into the silent house, making the old man laugh with his tricks and playfulness, following him around, rubbing against his legs. Dick wasn't lonely anymore, and I had watched a warm bond of friendship growing stronger over the years. In fact, it was something more — the old man seemed to depend on Frisk. And now this.*

Dick was not merely suffering from cancer, but Frisk suddenly blacked out. Though the cat recovered quickly, he suffered further worrying bouts of deep unconsciousness. Fortunately, this story has a happy ending, at least so far as the cat is concerned, for Herriot met the district nurse when she was delivering another dose of heroin and pethidine for the old man. Too shaky to take medicine straight from a bottle, Dick spooned it out from the saucer. The cat had lapped up the remains, putting it out for the count.

When Herriot visited the dying man in hospital, his last words (stroking the counterpane were 'Frisk ... Frisk'. At least he knew Frisk was well again; he had been found a good home.

Within days of arriving at its new home, a teeny ball of pale fluff, much of which seems to consist of a vibrator, so forceful is its half-developed purr, both conquers and is conquered by a man or woman who will never again be quite the same. The cat becomes wholly dependent on its human, a kind of surrogate mother figure, yet from the start it also knows its own mind and has instincts that nothing on earth can change. These things hold true despite the widest range of cat colourings, sizes, physiques, favourite foods, not to mention individual if not idiosyncratic behaviour. The humans (single or in families) and their approach to their cats are just as mixed. The limitless variations on a very standard theme are perhaps the whole point about cats. It is the very different relationships within such a seemingly inelastic framework that makes for much of the subject's fascination.

Creatures of habit yet prone to exotic one-off antics, individualists yet fitters-in, adventurers yet cautious survivors, cats display an enormous range of learning and ignorance. They treat themselves with deadly seriousness, yet are ever curious and great fun lovers. They are poor patients yet great survivors. They love their home, yet newspapers are full of accounts of them making long journeys. Paradoxes galore.

The question is whether we deserve the cats that live with us. Two things are certain. Many of us have discovered the cat to be the perfect pet. When you think about it, there aren't many alternatives beyond dogs, which don't suit the lifestyle of an increasing proportion of people living alone and/or working longer hours. We take longer and more adventurous holidays – and more of us live beyond being able to manage twice daily all-weather walks. Once dogs significantly outnumbered cats. Now it is reckoned that in the UK there are nearly 8 million cats, a number still increasing – one report says it has reached 9.2 million – against rather less than 7 million dogs. Over 5 million households have one or more cats. Unlike dogs, cats have no legal status, and figures cannot be precise.

Cats have never had it so good. A measure of that is their extended lifespan. As with humans, life expectancy has shot up since the war. Indeed one estimate suggests that in the last twenty years it has risen by as much as six years, from an average of ten to sixteen years. A dramatic change in the way they and we live is responsible. Even in the years immediately after the war, few people had more than a lone cat who was put out, or kept out, for considerable periods to fend for themselves. Cat flaps had yet to become popular. Before central heating, many cats would have been little warmer inside than out. They might have been loved, but it was hardly expected that family life would centre round them.

Many more households now have more than one cat, with examples of whole streets with more cats than humans.

Cats have adapted enormously ... especially to spending long periods by themselves in empty homes whose owners work longer hours and eat and socialise more outside the home. Once it was only Sunday morning that many cats spent alone; now Friday evenings are probably the loneliest time. Yes, cats give each other company but they still crave their humans.

With the merger of farms and closures of factories, far fewer cats are left to find their own food. Most cats now hunt for pleasure (or instinct). Even working cats have it easier. The job of 'official mouser' at the Famous Grouse distillery in Perthshire is now split between 'charismatic Dylan and the beautiful Brooke', a ginger-and-white tom and a semi-long-haired black-and-white female. Cats Protection took two months to select them to replace the legendary Towser who despatched 28,899 mice in her reign of all but a quarter of a century. Another short-listed candidate, Jet Li, was given a new home by a member of the distillery's staff.

Just as dramatic has been the change in our emotional approach to cats. Cat behaviourists – and who would have thought of them half a century ago? – emphasise how tolerant most of us have become. We expect our cats to rule us and may not check problem behaviour soon enough. Even in my childhood, most cats were entirely the responsibility of the woman of the house. Any petting by men would be surreptitious, out of public gaze. Now men are as free to show their emotions as women and children, and our actions haven't been slow to take advantage.

Another measure of change is the huge growth not only of the cat food business (a top line in supermarkets) but also of cat books and toys. Millions of pounds are spent on cats' Christmas presents, much of it sadly wasted. Many toys are just too ingenious. Few cats seem to be intrigued for more than a moment by wind-up ones. A realistic imitation mouse or ferret tossed near them often stimulates their own creativity, but often this blossoms best with a plain length of string or a scrunched piece of newsprint, a 'mouse' tossed around, 'lost' under a rug or chair, suddenly rediscovered and chased from a different angle.

One thing that has not changed is the influence of the class system. While the system itself might steadily evolve, it has always been fairly predictable what kind of people will have the most exotic cats, making a statement about their own social and financial position, and who will most spoil their cats.

As with so many other things in the class system, there is now more commonality in the approach to cats between the upper and working classes than with the variety of middle classes sandwiched in between. Though working people are feeling freer to be demonstrative, at the top and bottom generally cats are assumed to be a routine part of life, to be tolerated more than passionately loved. Aspirational middle-class folk are the most likely to have talkative Orientals and exotics. Cats are very special to many of them, a distinct part of life rather than routine. Because there are some cat-crazed people at all levels of society, generalisations are dangerous, yet it is the middle classes that mainly provide cat charities with the millions of pounds to keep them running.

Yet with their cats and many other things, middle class people are the great haters of waste and tightly control what they spend on their cats, which in all kinds of ways are less spoilt. Thus it is the cats most expensive to acquire who are mainly the very ones expected to eat up leftovers and are least likely to be welcomed on the bed. Working (and higher) class cats may be taken more for granted, but an essential part of that is the assumption they must do their own thing ... like rejecting cheaper brands of food and having the best chair by the fire.

The prospering of the working people has produced one major change, so fundamental that it affects the size of the future cat population, whose rapid growth in recent times may not be sustainable. Doctoring, or spaying, young cats was once shunned as too expensive, even if failure to do so resulted in unwanted kittens bringing their own cost. Noel Coward's 'You always ought to 'ave tom cats arranged, you know – it makes 'em so much more companionable' was addressed to a very select audience.

A vastly increased proportion of the population now visit vets (as they do indeed family clinics) so many fewer 'unwanted' kittens are born. The decrease in the number of farm cats (because so many small farms have disappeared) also contributes to the trend. Kittens that once might have been drowned because nobody wanted them are now in tight supply. When someone in our local town offered a single kitten free, he received 30 phone calls; vets are now asked to keep an ear out for any cats needing new homes. The cat population along with the human one is ageing, though as yet there are no cat pension plans for financial pundits to worry about.

If only cats could write about human foibles! Instead they simply adapt to make the best of what is on offer, ever ready to edge their way up the comfort scale. More and more of them fall on their feet ... as did a stray who walked into one of the National Trust's stately homes and instantly took on board an extensive territory and luxurious lifestyle.

Now to something on cats by W. H. Hudson that I read as a boy with Sam as a book rest on my lap. It is about London cats and surprises one far more today than it did 60 years ago.

At the end of the nineteenth century London was almost infested with cats, few of them kept as chosen pets. Most homes (small and crowded) had several, mainly transient strays living on scraps of food, often found in dustbins. Some actually lived in dustbins, little disturbed when warm ashes were thrown in. Anyone showing the slightest kindness attracted one or more like a magnet, though an open door was invitation enough. Recalling how much poorer the poor then were, it is worth quoting the passage's ending:

> *As a rule the animal prefers its own home with poverty to abundance in a strange place. I believe that a vast majority of these poor ones come from the houses or rooms inhabited by the poor. Most persons are extremely reluctant to put kittens that are not wanted to death. In the houses of the well-to-do the servants are ordered to kill them: but the poor have no person to delegate the dirty work to; and they have moreover, a kindlier feeling for their pet animals, owing to the fact that they live more with them in their confined homes than is the case with the prosperous. The consequence is that in very many cases*

not one of a litter is killed; they are mostly given away to friends, and their friends' children are delighted to have them as pets. The kitten amuses a child immensely with its playful ways, and is loved for its pretty blue eyes full of fun and mischief and wonder at everything. But when it grows up the charm vanishes, and it is found that the cat is in the way; he is often on the common staircase where there are perhaps other cats, and eventually he becomes a nuisance. The poor are also often moving, and are not well able to take their pet from place to place. It is decided to get rid of the cat, but they do not kill it, nor would they like to see it killed by another; it must be 'strayed' — that is to say, placed in a sack, taken for some miles away from home at night and released in a strange place.

In our time, at least that of older people, cats have achieved wondrous success in gaining economic progress and recognition at the centre of family life. But above all, our cats have helped free us to show our emotions.

So my wife Sheila sometimes asks which is the silliest: me holding an upside-down cat in my arms, stroking and talking to it, or the cat with wide-open blue eyes looking at me adoringly and purring away. Happily there is no answer. Both blades of the scissors cut; human and cat are free to make the best of each other.

Chapter 5

THE DESERT YEARS

Many of us regret those portions of our life, wasted years, when we were catless. After Lulu's departure I was without a cat at home for two decades. I was in catless digs, and my newspaper office, sole surviving building in the many acres of the bombed centre of Plymouth, was certainly no home for a cat. Hundreds of cats had been killed in the blitz, mostly unremembered since their owners went too. And a reporter's visits to people's homes were usually moments of tension when any cat would have been locked away.

Not that I consciously lamented the passing of better times – such as grammar school days where the plump tabby, much favoured by the cook, became a friend. Once she sat on my lap through the entire mathematics lesson taken by the headmaster who had arrived earlier than usual. Periodically he had noticed other pupils glancing in my direction and – not spotting the cat well hidden under my desk – came to examine just what I was doing. That was good for concentrating on the maths; my calculations were quickly completed. But I had to avoid stroking the cat and starting up her purr, and also had to ignore the pain she gave steadily, kneading my legs. Not an experience to be repeated, though the tabby continued to visit our classroom, dashing in through the door with a chirrup whenever possible. I forget her name but remember my surprise when she made a point of renewing friendship with a few favourite boys and girls at the start of each new term. I wondered how she updated her repertoire as old pupils disappeared and new juniors arrived at the change of the school year.

Married life began close to a particularly dangerous crossroads and, by the time we moved to a larger home, a farmhouse, a second child was planned. Much publicity was then given to babies being suffocated by cats warming themselves in prams, and anyway, fitting in book writing with a hectic journalistic and broadcasting career, and planning the launch of a publishing business while developing a serious fruit farm as a sideline, kept me more than busy.

Apart from which there was Henry, pronounced Eneri by the farm staff and our young daughter Alyss, who shrieked with joy, 'Eneri have come.' Having absented himself for days, even weeks, he came in a whirl, loudly announcing himself with his head held up toward heaven, or was it Dartmoor in the distance? After briefly rubbing himself against each of our legs, he lay in a seductive curve till approached, when he would set off on a hare-like circle, suddenly rushing to tap one of us on the ankle. Occasionally, with claw out, he drew blood. Part of Eneri's attraction lay in the fact that he was on forbidden territory. If his owner caught him on the wrong side of the fence, he would shout about how he had been robbed by our predecessor of living, home and tractor — and now we were taking his cat.

The fruit farm had been established by two friends who had shared the running of a division of South Indian

Railways before Indianisation of the management. After they and their wives had a monumental row, the holding was divided in two. We bought our house from the guy who had been divisional manager; his assistant manager had earlier been shown the door and settled in a former limekiln cut into the hill a hundred or so yards beyond the house. The farm staff shuddered at memories of the language when the former friends dumped dung at each other's doors.

Eneri belonged in the limekiln. Certainly that is where he was fed, though we thought he probably slept rough and had never been properly house trained. He begged to be let into our house, but once inside became desperately anxious to leave. Yet occasional appearances on the lawn showed that he obviously loved socialising and was full of fun – and surprises. He'd play for an hour, things usually ending when he became too excited and caught one of us with his claw out.

A handsome ginger with a pure white bib, Eneri was large and muscular. His front paws could be lethal. Any cat we had would probably have been given hell by him, or so we feared. Occasionally we heard awesome cat fights, and a tear in his ear or on his side would confirm his involvement. He must have been unneutered for in the spring he disappeared into distant territory for days at a time.

It was during one such spring that our neighbour stood in front of the tractor I was driving to ask accusingly if we had stolen Eneri too. 'He's not been around for a week. Are you sure you're not hiding him? Where else could he be?' As it happened, his absence was noted by one of the most distinguished publishers of all time, Allen Lane, founder of

Penguin, who happened to be related to the woman living in the converted limekiln and — to my personal disappointment — bought his (of course inferior) apples from them. Eneri's disappearance was once mentioned in a phone call, but unfortunately Sir Allen only really called me again to lobby for a job for his sister who lived locally. And I could hardly tell him of our neighbour's warped behaviour, often passing me without speaking but suddenly standing in front of the tractor I was driving to say that by rights it — and much more — belonged to him.

Eneri, bless him, helped keep the torch of feline infatuation alive, and certainly established our daughter as a lifelong cat lover. As he aged he became a sorrowful beast of the wild who probably never fully relaxed in comfort. He had disappeared from the scene years before our own cat, Sara, took over the territory and was instrumental in ending the enmity between limekiln and farmhouse. Our neighbours now made friendly telephone calls to ask if we minded Sara paying social visits. Cats don't only cause bad feeling by pooing in the fine tilth of a neighbour's seedbed, they also help settle old scores or encourage new friendships.

Naturally there were local cat encounters: not usually on walks through country lanes with plenty of dogs and wildlife but ne'er a cat, but occasionally in the village streets where someone would comment that I'd made a friend. Visits to my sister were enriched by Susie, a compact relaxed grey with a particularly quiet though determined voice. She was happy to be on anyone's lap provided she chose which, and was free to change her mind if she made an initial misjudgement. Susie actually belonged to my sister's daughter Naomi, diagnosed with terminal cancer soon after giving birth to her first child. Susie, who stayed with my sister, died of an illness before reaching a great age. Her memory, and the pleasure she gave, is still honoured. She did what cats are especially good at: being a gentle, loving diversion at times of tension.

Other relations and most friends were dog people or without any pet. We must have made the wrong kind of friends. Two colleagues with cats, who did steadily become friends, were the assistant and news editor of the regional daily I still worked for on an involved freelance basis. The first had a pair of slightly aloof moggies who didn't mind being picked up and put on your lap, but purred unenthusiastically and made little positive contribution apart from just being there and signalling contentment.

As befitted his character, the news editor had a more intense cat: nearly all black, handsome, harder to woo, more expressive when thawed, and needing frequent quick visits to the garden. She was most energetic and communicative when we toured the garden and reviewed the crops. Acting as though she were the chief inspector, always looking up but not quite at us as she darted about, never far in front or behind, she ensured the apples and pears didn't get all the attention.

How often I have seen people with the kind of cats they deserve, or even mirror images of themselves. Because cats are great fitters-in, we must conclude that our own cats living with different families wouldn't be at all the same. They make the fullest use of their physical surroundings and of human 'servants' prepared to indulge them so that owners' and felines' ways merge.

An artist colleague, designer of the David & Charles logo and illustrator of many books, not only had a large tabby, Titch, but also enjoyed drawing him. Titch was two cats in temperament. At some stage he'd obviously been wild or badly treated. He was choosy when he came indoors and cautious in what human company he accepted. Year after year, whenever I called he disappeared. Perhaps another tall man had once kicked him. It took a long time for Titch to realise it wasn't me. Only slowly do you come to understand how canny cats are at associating sounds, sight and actions as well as smells with individuals. However, Titch thawed as I became a frequent visitor. I announced my presence by pressing the doorbell (which gave the first ring) and holding it in for a few more seconds when it gave a second ring. Titch came to associate that with me, and expectantly waited for the door to be opened, when he'd run ahead to the chair in which I was to sit. My friend used two reception rooms and occasionally changed the furniture around, so the guidance could be useful. Trustingly, he looked into my eyes and generally considered I wasn't a bad proposition, which encouraged longer and more frequent visits. His home was a convenient stopping point on my way home, and anyway friendship deepened with his owners. Titch became the most reliable cat in my life at that time of great work pressure.

Then disaster. One day I had to return some artwork, and arrived carrying an attaché case. Titch saw it, gave me a look that implied 'you utter cheat, tricking me into accepting you' ... and was off. Whenever I visited thereafter, he disappeared. My attaché case was apparently just like that of the vet he detested; the mere sight of it destroyed our relationship. If only he could have stayed to sniff its difference from the vet's. It doesn't happen often, but with cats a misjudged association can spoil everything. Titch never again came to the door after my special ring, and though I only visited that one time with the attaché case, he always left the room if I came in.

A miscellany of cat encounters was offered by various forms of transport. A black cat with splendid sea legs could be met on the Scottish MacBrayne's steamer *King George V*, whose itinerary took it round the island of Mull in alternate directions on summer weekdays; most visitors to Iona went by it. The cat cheerfully conversed with passengers but gave the impression of being an important member of the crew, seldom away from one or more of them. I gathered that it had fun exterminating mice on board after each winter's lay-up. If you watched the ship unload its passengers at Oban at the day's end, it was sure to be by the gangway.

In those uncrowded days, sometimes a curious or hungry cat could be found making friends with other passengers waiting for an infrequent ferry before being swept up by its owner and put back in his car. Then many people carried their cats loose in cars; you could be amused by the antics of one in the back window of the vehicle ahead of you, and might possibly meet it if you stopped for a rest in a lay-by or car park. The more casual lifestyle and the smaller scale of things didn't isolate us from other people's pets as has happened since. You'd hardly expect to find a friendly cat in service stations or supermarkets, but family grocers usually had one asleep in the window, socialising on a chair or chasing a real or pretend mouse around the floor. Such cats were usually well fed, if not oversize, suggestive of the good things their shop sold.

More people travelled by train with their cats, usually kept in boxes with a small aperture. The first time I remember eyeing one for several hours was during the 1938 Munich crisis, when an earlier start to World War II was only narrowly averted. Thousands of passengers and their belongings crowded into trains bound for the safety of the West Country. Even in post-war years there was often a boxed or caged cat on the seat opposite staring at you and perhaps meowing inquisitively.

There were many station cats – a few of them famous such as the Paddington cat – who made the most of the coal fires in the booking office and waiting room. There were fires in signal boxes, too. While more signalmen brought their dogs along to keep them company, a few shared their duty with a cat. A lover of everything to do with railways, I used to be allowed unofficially to work a range of country boxes and especially enjoyed a tortoiseshell cat waking from a long sleep for a snack and cuddle before trotting down the outside steps for a touch of hunting and call of nature. As with the signalmen's dogs, the cats seemed to understand the working of the box sufficiently to know when their owner's duty came to an end, and uncannily were always eagerly waiting to leave at the considerably earlier Saturday changeover time arranged to give the signalman a long weekend at the end of his early-shift week.

It was in 1970, when I was 40, that a transatlantic westbound voyage on the *QE2* carrying many emigrants was enlivened by a twice-daily visit to the kennels on an upper deck where a lone tabby among half a dozen dogs about to start life in a new continent instantly welcomed attention. Sniffing what little it could of me through the netting, its conversation ended in a crescendo of pleading high-pitched almost inaudible meows. 'Oh please take me out of this basket. Why am I here? I deserve better — don't you agree? Take me please.'

It was only when I went for a farewell conversation on the last morning as we approached the Statue of Liberty through a misty thunderstorm that I was told that only people with pets there should visit the kennels. Crossing the Atlantic in the following years, I sometimes wondered how that lonely tabby made out in his new land. His owner was never around on my visits.

During my first fortnight on publishing business in the States, mainly in New York itself, I only saw two cats — the first indoor ones yet met. In that environment, obviously cats couldn't safely roam, but was it fair to have a cat at all? When I knelt to talk to a tabby at the first home I visited, the host almost pulled me up saying, 'You don't need to bother with that ... come and have a cocktail.' My second host was a gentleman publisher, delighted that I noticed and spoke to his cat, another but more distinguished tabby beautifully fitting into the literary atmosphere. Exuding presence, watching us converse and then putting in its dime's worth, it would have been at home with the greatest. So here was at least one happy indoor cat.

I have never seen a cat in a North American hotel, but visits to British ones were another source of cat encounters. It was actually the brief — albeit in a few cases recurring — friendships with hotel cats that increasingly made me feel there was a hole in my life. Possibly hotels with cats are less hygienic, but by its very existence a cat at rest on the best seat in front of the fire spells a warmer welcome than the formula greeting hoteliers use to welcome their guests and assure them of their best attention.

'Put that cat out of the way' – one guest instructing the other, usually the wife to husband – shows that hotels don't always have the right kind of guests. Is it not a sin to turn off a sleeping cat? The challenge is to talk to it as though you are a long-lost friend desperate for its company. I love watching a cat so approached slowly wake up, yawn, close its eyes, yawn again, and again, stand up, tentatively stretch its legs, stretch them again with further yawn, and then slowly approach, sniffing to see if you are as friendly as you sound. That confirmed at leisure, with more yawning and scratching, the cautious approach continues, sometimes developing into such friendship that you might surreptitiously be followed to your bedroom or the dining room – until of course the hotel staff intervene if they happen to be around. They usually aren't ... as too often we discover if we actually need someone. Cats following you to your bedroom are great fun, but what do you do when they come to check the minibar?

Emphasising the point that more humans now think it acceptable to show emotion, a much larger proportion of hotel guests accept a cat's presence and make friendly overtures than was the case 30 or more years ago. Conversely, many private hotels have been bought by chains whose rules and budgets exclude felines.

It was at the The Elms Hotel at Abberley in England's Worcestershire, where the family was taking a rare luxury night, that I first became aware of the peculiar attraction of Burmese. The afternoon had been memorable, firstly for the waiter placing a succession of china bowls containing individual portions of selected vegetables on the burner until each loudly cracked. Then my son Gareth, perhaps six at the time, was upset. He had been forced to choose something more original from the menu than fish and chips and, when released after pud, went straight to his room to phone room service to order fish and chips, which the hotel of course didn't send. So, when we met after snooze time, he announced, 'This is a very bad hotel. It pretends to offer room service, but it doesn't.' After that, when he demanded a game of croquet on the lawn, we naturally acquiesced.

At the first sound of wood on wood, mallet on ball, a brown Burmese burst out of the lounge door, pompously announced himself, and started to pull out the winning post. Then, accurately gauging our sight line, he demolished successive hoops by circling them with his substantial body and levering them upwards with tremendous kicking of his rear legs.

Gareth was all for bypassing the hoop with the cat round it and going straight to the next. The Burmese instantly cottoned on to that. Whether you're at your desk, reading in bed or playing croquet, cats know exactly what you are looking at. So the cat won the game. All four of us gathered round admiringly.

My son, never one to leave a tool idle, hit a ball nonchalantly. Exactly what the Burmese wanted. He spent the next half hour chasing and redirecting balls, preferably two at a time. He then rolled on his back. Once we had stroked his tummy he made a speech, which we took to mean it was time for afternoon tea in the lounge and he'd pick the best lap.

Cats are a bit like aches and pains. Given half an excuse, people tell you about theirs. They usually boast of the most wonderful cat the world has ever seen. It's a lot more entertaining than hearing about slipped discs, arthritis and digestive upsets. With the Burmese settling for Gareth's lap, one couple asked what cats we had. None, but we were thinking about getting one, a moggie.

'Oh you should have one of these, or a Siamese. I couldn't be without one.'

'Aren't they very demanding?' we enquired.

'As friendly as a dog, a lot cleaner, less destructive and, well, responsive pets. They relate to everyone in the family ... in fact, family life often revolves round ours.'

I never saw that huge, brown Burmese again, but have often thought about him, and felt the dancing pace of his ghost wandering round the hotel when I returned a generation later. But it was he who inspired us — or was it gave us the confidence? — to think of having an Oriental. At that stage I am ashamed to say I'd never touched a practical or breed cat book; even the first basic guide to owning a cat now further opened up the mysterious, fascinating world I had already begun exploring.

Soon, furtively at first, and then shared with the family, I read the classified 'Kittens for Sale'. Alyss wanted them all; Gareth the most boisterous-sounding ones; me the most outgoing one in the world.

Still feeling an Oriental might be too demanding, we started — badly — with successive moggies.

There is only the dimmest of memories of the first, who

had non-stop enteritis from which the vet said he wouldn't recover. We should have bought him from a better home.

The second was a charmer. Though his ginger fur was short, when he accidentally got shut out in a rainstorm one realised it accounted for much of his visual size. There seemed to be nothing to his body beyond emotion and fun. His tail wasn't even a decent piece of string, his paws minute, though able to move far faster than your eye could follow.

Straight from his mum, on arrival he instantly concluded that we were where he belonged and that we were a good thing. Though hungry, he was far more demanding of love. I had to wait 40 years to have another cat who looked so directly, imploringly, lovingly, into my eyes. He'd climb up my legs and tuck himself into my jacket for a warm purr. Then, to make sure that my voice really did belong to me, he'd come up my tie to check my face. When still at less than three months, he'd fall asleep anywhere on me, but never missed getting to the toilet in time. His meow was a lot less developed than his purr, and we could only imagine what kind of grown-up voice he might have had, for one morning we came down to find him unconscious under the ironing board. In some nocturnal prank, he had brought it down on himself.

What feeling of guilt. How often since I have furtively made sure that any ironing board I pass in a home with a cat is securely fastened. Though I cannot recall the little treasure's name, I still relive the anxious days waiting to see if he would come out of his coma. After the rest of the family had gone to bed, I would stroke him and talk soothingly just in case he might open his eyes. Never a flicker. A lost cause, said the vet, whose invoice had a second line added under the photocopy of the first: Kitten PTS (put to sleep).

In those days, it was not uncommon to receive photocopied bills, with new items added under those already charged and paid for until the whole sheet was filled. For years after we had Sara, the cost of her treatment came on bills whose first two lines gave us the grim reminder (as though we could possibly have forgotten):

> Kitten PTS
> Kitten PTS

Our sorrow was matched by determination to do better and education that included more reading and visits to several cat shows — a delightful way to spend a few Saturday mornings, finally learning just how varied cats are in appearance, temperament and voice.

The shows also provided interesting and informative talk with the officials who had organised them, and with the exhibitors, the cat owners, some of them breeders. Comparing thoughts with the owners, including local folk I already knew, I realised that cat people are different ... something emphasised as we later began publishing cat books. Yes, on balance they are a bit not catty but scatty. At the shows, some of them seemed reluctant to finish a sentence before darting to a new topic, also left in mid-air. Yet they were delightful. Ever since then, with hundreds if not thousands of examples, I have come seriously to believe that cat owners are nicer than average humans. They have a better-balanced value system, and in particular are less dictatorial in their manner and view. Governments might be less determined, but would be a lot closer to the people, if they were formed entirely of cat lovers.

It is perhaps strange that so many famous publishers have been cat lovers, for to make an impact in publishing you have to be pretty determined ... though not so much to make money as to publish good books. It is perhaps that value placed on standards and reputation as opposed to wealth that made most traditional family publishing houses happier than average businesses. Today's cut-throat competition for profit has certainly made publishing a less desirable career for those who are not financially single-minded, so that no doubt fewer cat lovers are found in editorial and marketing teams.

I came so strongly to believe that cat lovers couldn't be bad people that, after reading my first personal cat book ever, I made allowances for the snub I'd received from its author. A. L. Rowse was known to be a peppery Cornishman and Oxford academic, yet that scarcely prepared me for his put down. When I asked if he might be interested in writing a Cornish book for David & Charles, he replied that if ever he was reduced to writing a history of Truro Grammar School, if no other were interested, he might just possibly consider me a suitable publisher.

In his *Peter, the White Cat of Trenarren*, he says revealingly that as a child, when he sometimes cried, it would be a 'little cat who would put an arm and paw around my head and nurse me, with true maternal instinct – which is more that my mother ever did'. Later in life, as a bachelor, he regarded his white fluffy Peter as the most precious possession he had ever had. It is a touching tale, later reprinted in *Three Cornish Cats* and – breaking largely untilled ground — sold astonishingly well. But then his *A Cornish Childhood* sold 400,000 copies, a success impossible in today's crowded book market.

Between the pepper-potted references to his own status, Rowse charmingly describes how Peter arrived as a three-quarter-grown stray — 'a rather gangling adolescent, with a way of holding his tail on one side which I didn't much like' — and how they became close to each other, especially enjoying games just before bedtime. Usually these involved make-believe mice: 'about pretending, about acting in inverted commas'. In the morning 'down he would come, jump on the bed, mount on my chest and bite me gently on the chin.' So Rowse wasn't all pomp and status.

Rowse introduced me to other writers, including Thomas Hardy, who had been passionate about their own special cats and mourned their demise. This cat thing was giving a new perspective to life itself. At the next cat show, I was amazed how the cats made sure that the humans, though very much needed, were only the sideline. It was a *cat* show. Even the timid, hating the public stare, some of them hidden behind a courtesy cloth, had presence, often a beautiful statuesque one. Naturally we went for the cats that screamed for our attention. If I leant against the netting, several climbed up my jacket. What bundles of joy! And how well they coped with being shut for hours in a cage with even their toilet on full view.

My heart was especially won by one Siamese kitten, infinitesimal yet with grand stature and great confidence. Through the netting, she climbed up my jacket and nibbled my small finger. When unable to get closer, she dropped to the cage's bottom to roll pleadingly, again quickly coming up my jacket and repeating the process several times over. Then the breeder arrived. 'She's very special.' An exchange of glances with my wife confirmed she would be our immediate choice. But she was already bespoke, though it might have been that the breeder had decided to keep her himself.

Along the corridor, a blood-curdling sound was coming from a fully-grown Siamese. We recognised it as being similar to a fearful utterance on the terrace outside our bedroom some years before. Then we were too afraid to go and see what wild creature was clamouring for attention. Now we realised we had rejected the overtures of a harmless cat wishing to visit us, maybe having lost its way and in need of help. What fools we can feel because something is unfamiliar to us. A Siamese crying out like that is probably never heard by the vast majority of humans so — we asked ourselves, now feeling guilty — how were we to know it wasn't something dangerous and better ignored? Whose cat it might have been we never had any idea.

After several cat shows, there was no doubt about it. Siamese seemed especially responsive. The time had come to take the final plunge.

Why hadn't we reached this point earlier?

Chapter 6

SARA

In Chapter 1 I described how Sara nudged my finger when the family went to select our kitten from a Siamese litter. Ten days later, in the evening when the children were in bed, I went to collect her. As soon as she saw me, she walked boldly towards me, liked being picked up and being pressed against my cheek. From the start she thought it fun being put into the travelling cage. On the way home, however, she insisted I held her paw. Each withdrawal of my left hand to change gear resulted in mega wailing, which ceased instantly I re-established physical contact.

Arriving at her new home, she jumped out of the cage, explored the room and climbed up my trousers. I'd obviously become her new mother figure. She seemed to be instantly at ease, trusting ... until an involuntary cough made her leap, turn in mid-air and face me, hissing into my face, her scraggy piece of string of a tail bushed out in fury. Sorry. Sorry. Sorry. Miraculously she understood. Trust was restored. Always after 'Sorry' put her at her ease. Providing it was not too painful, she liked having me accidentally step on her because 'Sorry' meant she had my undivided attention. Later she keenly accepted 'Sorry' from for any of us, anybody.

A little later, she was taken to the kitchen and shown her food, water and litter tray. She ate a little food and found her own way back to the lounge, again climbed up my trousers and switched on her purr. 'You are mine. I belong to you which gives you great responsibility.' After much discussion, it was agreed she would sleep by herself near the Aga, which instantly belonged to her too. If she cried in the night we wouldn't have heard her, but half an hour after settling her I went back and found her fast asleep curled up as close as possible to the Aga in what then seemed her ridiculously large new bed.

At six-thirty, when I went downstairs, she was crying, but purred immediately and followed me ... upstairs for the first time. Stairs were a new experience. She was so tiny that she had to claw her way up them one at a time. She ate, drank water, used her litter tray, explored the house up and down, and spent much of the time on my desk fascinated by the typewriter until she fell asleep. Later in the day she spent time on the laps of my wife and our children Alyss and Gareth, happy with each but especially so tucked under my jacket while we laughed at *Dad's Army*, whose signature tune she came to love since it meant the whole family would be relaxed around her. She loved us all being together.

Within two days of arrival she had demonstrated that she was ready for a new home, liked all of us but had decided I would be her greatest devotee, knew how to accept 'Sorry', about eating, drinking and lavatorial arrangements. She knew she would be fed by my wife, chase the children and the string they trailed behind them ... and be extremely adaptable yet a creature of fixed habits knowing exactly where she fitted on my left-hand bosom. She slept a lot, yet knew immediately if someone was at the door, was intrigued by what lay beyond the windows and mad at the very sight of birds, which she always chatted at, despising them as mice or voles cheating with wings. For her mini stature, and with such a scrimpy tail, she sometimes treated herself with deadly seriousness, but she enjoyed fun and even my laughter when she caught me unawares by tapping my nose. She soon understood that the telephone couldn't be ignored, but expected us to resume whatever we were doing once the receiver was replaced. Only once, during a particularly long call, did she try to snatch the receiver, which was regarded as the nuisance, not me.

I also learnt a bit more about my place in the universe and that, unique though he may be, man is only one of God's creatures. You could not but respond with an upwelling of love and enthusiasm for life. As Albert Schweitzer put it: 'Human dignity depends on respect for all living creatures.' (More specifically he said, 'There are two means of refuge from the miseries of life: music and cats.') Loving Sara meant better respecting other animals and insects, even if she hunted them.

It has already been mentioned that people often seem to have the cats they deserve. Partly this is because of choice of kitten; for example, timid people going for a retiring kind of cat. Those who have led hard lives themselves frequently pick a kitten or (more likely in their case) an adult cat with inherent problems. When there were so many cats seeking new homes, was it selfish going for a lively lass of a kitten? To a degree probably, yes, for though prepared — inevitable isn't it? — to nurture my cat, I'm not sure it is sensible for people to dedicate their lives to a lost cause. I have seen several friends weighed down with problem dogs as well as cats; misery all round. Once or twice I have thought that on balance it would have been better for them to change their pet. While I hate the thought of putting down any living thing, a human's happiness is perhaps more important? Controversial ground; many animal lovers may not agree. If there is a message it must be to take care when we select a pet — and especially if we add a second or third cat to the family, for cats are not naturally social and extended cat families are risky.

We had booked to go on a short break a few weeks later, and had bought Sara on condition the breeder would take her back while we were away. She seemed too small and precious to be sent to a cattery. But it was a mistake, and I guess the breeder shouldn't have agreed. Sara's mum wasn't at all pleased to see her; she made it very plain she wasn't wanted. I have learnt since that queen cats forget their offspring if separated for more than a couple of weeks, so Sara was probably given the cold shoulder any strange cat would have received.

Somewhat lighter, for she hadn't eaten much, Sara was delighted to be in the cage on the way home again, yowling at the same traffic lights when I had to take my hand away from her to change gear. I'm sure she wondered why I hadn't progressed to automatic transmission. Thereafter she only went on holiday to my wife's parents, about which more anon. She never saw a cattery.

At home she did all that could be expected and more. Daily she explored every room, became a distinct creature of habit, took part in every family occasion and chose her favourites from among visitors. Of course she ignored scratching posts, learnt that she could get attention by attacking the furniture, and loved the satisfaction of wrecking the cork on the bathroom stool. Through the cat flap, whose working she cottoned on to immediately, she steadily explored more widely. From kittenhood to old age, whichever of us called her, she'd come back though, if hunting far away, in leaps and bounds, sometimes across ploughed fields, perhaps in fifteen minutes, with or without game. She probably had a lively female cat's typical 15-acre 'territory'; adventurous males have larger areas they know intimately.

As mentioned elsewhere, though they take no part in parenthood, it is the father who determines most of a cat's character; friendly fathers produce happy, inquisitive kittens. Sara's dad must have been an outgoing chap getting involved in everything around him.

One afternoon I was working in a field while Sara was in the lane beyond the vole-infested hedge. I could just see a mum come along holding her child. For some reason, local legend had it that Siamese were dangerous — a belief as silly as many other rural legends, often restricted to small localities, are. Sara was then barely nine months old. 'Don't go near that one,' said Mum, guiding the child away. 'They get you, them do. Dangerous things.' Sara instinctively respected two-legged mammals, and steadily built up a wide circle of two-legged friends, while regarding all four-legged beasts along with birds as inferior beings to be ridiculed or hunted.

Was she as perfect as Patrick Moore, one of my authors, always thought his cat was? Patrick claimed his Jeanie had an especially gentle nibble for his toes sticking out beyond the duvet. Once our cats even corresponded. But then Sara always had birthday and Christmas cards and presents. Cats allegedly writing to each other must bring millions in extra revenue for the postal service.

Sara seemed a strong character yet, when we thought it might be a good thing to give her company, since we were all away with long working and school days, she immediately played second fiddle to a fluffy white girl kitten. It was the baby newcomer who led the way upstairs first in the morning. Sara tracked her every move. Alas, the kitten had severe health problems — we discovered the whole litter had been affected — and quickly appeared as another line, 'Kitten PTS', on the vet's bill. Sara didn't seem to miss her, and we didn't repeat the experiment of giving her feline companionship. No doubt relationships would have been very different had we been a two-cat family, but Sara was everything you could wish a sole cat to be.

A happy standard chocolate-point spayed Siamese, her nose, ears and paws became steadily darker as she grew from a wisp of a kitten to a substantial cat. Her action- and emotion-packed life of 21 years took me from my early thirties to mid-fifties, the years one is supposed to do it all. Whatever I achieved, she helped, a constant companion in good times and bad.

Dog lovers sometimes point out that a cat only does what it wants, not what a self-respecting canine feels obliged to do. Yes, a dog's friendship and service, like that of a slave, is more reliable. A dog may be the one unselfish friend that man can have. But do we humans have special dispensation only to expect to please ourselves and be pleased? Is a cat's freely given love less valuable because it isn't turned on as automatically as water coming out of a tap? Sara loved me because she wanted to, her love often overcoming her natural instinct. Yet instinct was never far away. Apart from the first drives home, when she needed to be held for comfort and reassurance, she never let me hold her front paw in case she had to make a quick dash for it. But, both of us realising there were times that weren't convenient for each other, we were on a far more equal footing than man and dog.

Naturally there were a few problems. She was curious about the chimney, and one day looked as though she might try to jump up it over glowing ashes. Fearful she'd burn herself, I jumped up from the piano I was playing and showed unusual fury. Ever after, when I played the piano she thought she had to go to the chimney. She became so besotted with me that when my daughter and I fooled around together, she had to take my side and bit (not very successfully) my daughter's legs.

The vet thought she was a cat from hell. 'Oh that she-devil again.' The vet's assistant was utterly unable to hold her; under stress her wriggling, especially the back paws, developed enormous force. It was just about possible for me to coax her and hold all four paws locked together in my cupped hands, and even then she bit the vet. 'She-devil. Why on earth did you choose her?'

She avoided swallowing pills with extraordinary cunning. If you could get one into her mouth and thought she'd actually swallowed it, five minutes later up it would come.

'Damnation,' shouted the vet. 'Compared with her, a sick horse is a walkover. Shall I give you the dates I'm on holiday so she can have her treatment then?'

Yet, the cage left open, when freed she jumped straight in and purred away. Even when she might have guessed we were taking her to the vet, the moment the cage was opened, in she jumped. Moments of tension were pronounced but short. If something made her petrified there was no build up to it, and relaxation followed naturally. How stupid, I thought, for we humans to build up fear of going to the dentist and worrying about dangers that have passed. Compared with cats, we seem to glorify anxiety.

Sara looked after herself well and had only one risky habit. She took on many dogs, and loved nothing better than to stay up a post until a familiar Labrador passed, when she'd leap onto its back and swing from its tail. But if a dog ran towards her, instead of seeking safety up the nearest tree or post, she'd run all the way home. She was fast, and only once did a dog almost catch her by the tail.

Looking back to those days before most cars had seat belts we ourselves were foolish, driving the 30 miles to and from my parents-in-law's house on the outskirts of Dartmoor with her loose. Mercifully, she never got under my feet, or was thrown by a sudden stop. She spent most of her time on the back window ledge attracting the attention of following motorists. She scarcely made a sound until she recognised we were towards the journey's end when she began demanding she be the first to be let out. When we read about the dangers of having a loose cat in the car, she adapted instantly to going in her cage, but — though she couldn't see — still sensed when we were nearing the end of the journey.

From the start, when still only a few months old, Sara took to the idea of spending occasional time in my parents-in-law's rambling old mansion, whose grounds she fully explored. At three breakfasts running, she brought in a pigeon's egg and batted it across the kitchen floor, a hatched bird appearing the fourth morning.

When a bungalow was being built for my parents-in-law on the edge of our fruit farm, she waited until the last of the builders had left to examine their day's work, spending longer with us on Saturday mornings, jumping between walls when we reviewed the week's progress. She especially enjoyed exploring rafters as the roof took shape, descending to ground level sure-footed, backwards, by ladder. After Granny and Grandad (as the whole family called them) moved in, she frequently went by leaps and bounds across the fields to pay a social visit. After supper, if I walked down by the lane, she'd come with me ... unless it was wild weather when she'd go to the car and shriek at the top of her voice for a lift.

She built up different relationships with different members of the extended family, but kept a special controlling eye on me. She taught me how to relax. I'd always frowned when having my photograph taken until I came to look natural with her in my arms. Perhaps that is why so many people are pictured with their cats.

She knew all about the working week. Before we even saw her in the morning, she beyond doubt knew when it was Saturday. But that isn't unusual. Gizmo is a large ginger Persian cat in the Scottish town where we now live who walks with his owner through the woods, but stays in bushes while he crosses a busy road to buy a newspaper. That is on

Mondays to Saturdays. Though the owner goes at the same time and swears he gives no clue about it being Sunday, the cat crosses the road with him to fetch the *Sunday Post*. And ginger-and-white Domino, who spends virtually all his time at Hampstead's Heath Library when it is open, always leaves shortly before its varied closing time without instruction or (so says the librarian) any clue.

My prolonged trips overseas on publishing business were a different matter. Like most cats, Sara quickly noticed telltale preparations and looked morose. On my return she'd try to punish me. Once she successfully sent me to Coventry for several whole days. On my return from an especially long trip, she walked away, head high, tail limply tucked under her rear end, the epitome of the sulking cat ... only to return seconds later, her pride beaten, making a hideously emotional cacophony and leaping a couple of yards into the arms she assumed would catch her. Greetings were always accompanied with a lick on the nose.

On my return from a long trip, I had to hear about her latest hunting exploits. Voles were everyday, so riddled were the orchards with them. Field mice happily rarer; one got clean away having surprised her with a brave display of boxing. Rabbits and birds, from partridges to pigeons as well as small garden birds (but the friendly pheasant always escaped), were fairly routine 'gifts'. A hare and a squirrel were very unusual, grass snakes only a couple of times — mercifully never an adder — and only once a stoat.

The stoat, sleek and white, had just been dumped in the children's brick box while we were trying to eat breakfast when a farmer arrived by tractor asking if he might fill the tank on his trailer with our water. 'Certainly,' we said, 'but could you first help us eject the stoat.'

'Sooner you than me.' He drove off as though we had the plague. Frightened, the stoat was a fierce adversary, which Sara now sensibly left alone. In its wriggling, it managed to bite the thumb of one of the gloves we used, mercifully missing our flesh. No sooner was it put out than a stray dog walked into the kitchen. That Sara wasn't going to allow, but on the slippery linoleum she made no progress in chasing it. The two animals, eight paws peddling rapidly, effectively stood still, so that after the stoat it was a doddle to catch Sara and shoo the dog away. It was not a peaceful breakfast.

When a sheep broke out of its field to eat the greener grass of our lawn, we found it easy to lead the way back — until it screamed and jumped in agonised circles as Sara mounted its back and swung vigorously from the poor thing's tail. That was one of the moments we could have strangled her. Others were when she woke us up by yowling on the terrace; disappearing into thin air and ignoring our calls when she was only feet away enjoying the fun; creating an instant jumbled mess when a hank of wool was being wound; struggling through the cat flap with a mutilated hare just as my taxi arrived to take me on the first stage of a sales trip round the world.

One afternoon, such was the hurry for a BBC radio car to get back to the studio that a mike was held out of its window, the interviewer's terrier also leaning out while I answered questions crouched on the tarmac. What the urgent broadcast was about has been lost in memory, but how vividly I recall watching Sara. It was too much to expect her to leave us alone! Seeing the dog, she dashed into the hedge, returning with a vole that she tossed in the air. It nearly hit the mike. It made the terrier bark furiously. Cats are exhibitionists by nature, but this was ridiculous – and expensive. It cost me a minute's broadcast fee since I'd saved a titbit of information to take the interview over the three minutes that the minimum payment covered. The instant the dog barked, thinking she had enough material, the interviewer roared away down the drive, saving the BBC a quarter of the money I had expected.

Sara wouldn't be left out of anything. When daffodils fluttered in the wind, she'd gather large bunches of them in her front paws. Every bed, every parcel was hers. Tea towels over the Aga rail made nice bedding. If we threw something to each other, naturally it was assumed to be for her benefit. Like most cats, she didn't know the difference between ours and hers, so anything loose in the kitchen was fair game – but she never begged at meal times. She knew her name, though thought 'Cat' more endearing, and understood 'Sorry', 'Soon', 'Come', 'Hot' (wait for food to cool), 'Fire' (to sit by), 'Comfy' (a bed on a cold night), 'Garden' (a saunter round the garden) and (like a dog) 'Walk' down the lane ... and in later years even 'Car'.

Of course she was marvellous and, except for the inevitable perversity of always being on the wrong side of the door and demanding it be opened, she was as co-operative as the kids (and they weren't bad).

Beside my typewriter, her velvet paw occasionally playing with the keys, she surely helped both relax me and increase productivity. She'd seldom speak except when spoken to. She wasn't a great one for looking into your eyes – for that I had to wait decades longer – but if you spoke to her, blinking heavily, occasionally closing your eyes, she'd close hers and pump up the purr, though that was always loudest when upturned in my arms in the evening.

She was a fussy, aristocratic eater. Like many cats, she needed variety. Though she had her favourites, they could be offered too frequently – except for pheasant, for which she was always game. She showed disapproval by walking away from her dish, vigorously shaking her right rear paw. Things off our plates were more prestigious than mere cat food. Before we learnt that dairy produce is generally bad for cats, she'd spend half an hour chasing a near-empty cream carton around the kitchen lino, repeatedly pushing her paw into it and licking it. In her later years we developed a ritual of her only being fed if she jumped up into my waiting arms. After a few typical feline delays, such as having to scratch her ear, this she unfailingly did. That delayed the moment of truth, seeing her either tuck in or walk away shaking her back right paw.

When my wife and I split up, it was planned that Sara would spend a last evening in the empty farmhouse. She wasn't having that, and demanded to be let in by Granny and Grandad, who were delighted she'd chosen them. That was the last time she walked between homes, or indeed out of the (smaller) garden of my new home.

So much had Granny and Grandad come to adore Sara, that when they moved into an annex of their daughter's home they were delighted that her two Burmese spent most of the time in their room. We will meet them in the next chapter.

Had we stayed in the farmhouse, she would undoubtedly have continued distant explorations, but her decision (if it was a conscious one) never to go beyond the new garden limits didn't seem to age her. She adjusted instantly to her new home, and found plenty of wildlife and diversions in the garden – including the new experience of watching fish in a pond. The fish were safe since she would never get her paw wet. She hated water. Until almost the end of her life I took her to Granny and Grandad, now ex-parents-in-law, whom she greeted with much fuss and the repertoire of pranks she'd uniquely developed for their benefit. She was still learning new tricks when she turned twenty. Suddenly she started yodelling with a powerful tremolo. With astonishment, I first heard it on a telephone call from Australia. 'What on earth's that?' I demanded. The answer: 'Your cat protesting you're not talking to her.' She purred at my voice when I did speak, which happened regularly. And international phone calls were expensive in those days.

When 21, slow and having lost the spring that allowed her to jump from the floor to my arms as a ritual at feeding time, she still kept her dignity, affectionately licked my nose and purred greatly. Now she scarcely wanted to leave my side, my mere presence spelling security. Purring no doubt helped her as well as me. But she still wouldn't let me hold her paw. Though at the end she might not have moved had a mouse passed by, her instinct told her always to be free.

One morning when she was well into her twenty-second year, after feeling the final purr and saying goodbye, with her accusingly looking as though she understood it all, I went to work knowing that the vet who continued to call her a she-devil would come and put her peacefully to sleep. Her kidneys were failing, destroying her self-respect. How I dreaded going back that evening, seeing her claw marks on the bathroom stool, the empty space in front of the Aga.

Sara taught me much about both her own species and myself, helped liberate me from uptightness and prevented me from taking my staff for granted. Mind you, it was said that to get on at David & Charles you had to be a cat lover. The board meetings of our American branch in a Vermont farmhouse were virtually chaired by Ying, who taught me that Siamese appreciate a good spank just in front of the tail. After initial surprise, Sara loved it — as do my current Balinese.

Finally, Sara taught me to grieve, which I did more fully and naturally than when rarely seen relatives died. She undoubtedly made me a better person: not a bad reason for having a cat.

Sara vividly lives on in the memory of several of us, appears in many photographs, and was the subject of my most commented on column in the regional morning paper: a loving obituary on the first anniversary of her death. Many readers said they had cut it out to help them when the time came for them to lose their own cat. 'The love of a great cat never dies,' said one of them. It certainly hasn't been extinguished yet.

Now for another perspective. My son Gareth, has his own — selective? — recollections of Sara. I think his memory is a bit off but have resisted the temptation to edit the sentiments. Gareth is a publisher in Australia, also with a New Zealand company, and is enthusiastically publishing this book in both countries, as he did my recent *Journey*

Through Britain: Landscape, People and Places, which also includes cat encounters. There is, for instance, Grace, the apricot and pale grey who showed us round the historical garden at the Dower House of the former Benedictine Morville Hall in Shropshire, and the hospitable Siamese Fuffino who loves to be swung by his tail. (His owner has just reported how he entered a neighbour's kitchen, opened the upright deep freeze and, unable to get into the drawers, stalked off leaving the door open and the food to perish. Her own small fridge had to be fitted with a 'kiddie lock' after he was observed opening it, removing two fish – taking one for himself and generously allowing Toby, the large Border Collie, the other.)

Gareth writes:

> Sara, my father's cat, for she was no one else's, looked after the mice, birds, neighbouring sheep and a couple of kids on her extended territory. It was a demanding job. Dad assisted her at weekends and Sara assisted Dad with his evening meetings with the miscellany of personalities involved in his publishing enterprise. So let us go back in memory …
>
> Business has been good and the throaty growl of Dad's new car is heard coming up the lane. The house goes into a well-practised ritual. Mother disappears. My sister takes up a position on the upstairs balcony so she can pretend to be passing as Dad's visitor arrives. She has discovered boys and is ever hopeful. Some of the visitors are of the age that a fifteen-year-old girl could dream about, but they all seem more interested in her father than her. Just by chance I happen to be

outside so fortuitously can be an early judge of the visitor's character. Sara wakes up, slowly limbering down from the airing cupboard and stretching her way downstairs. She reaches the second lowest step, safely hidden from the entrance, just as the door opens.

Dad shouts 'hello' as visitor walks in and there is a general fussing. To take his coat off visitor has to face upstairs and so sees sister. Visitor hangs up coat as sister's door bangs shut. Mother comes along corridor from the kitchen and seems surprised to see visitor, Dad and me there; she was actually looking for the cat. Sara isn't in a mood to know who 'the cat' is and accordingly isn't found.

The lounge door opens and (when nearly closed) the streaking white Sara, still unseen by visitor, enters. The fire is probably alight. Mother produces some nice refreshments and the conversation begins to turn to business. By now Sara has fully sized up the visitor and taken the initial tactical decision. As to purpose and strategy, well that is obvious: get this person to agree with Dad. And remember, if Dad attacked sister (in fun) Sara did so too (seriously). Nobody should disagree with him.

Sara seldom misreads the visitor. A glamorous woman is waving her legs around and suddenly protests about her stockings being ripped. The incredibly nasty-looking financial fellow comes with a self-important leather case that Sara uses as a scratching post. Tactics are, however, generally kinder — if you exclude jumping on to a large, earnest if not pompous author with papers on his lap, teacup in one hand and sticky bun in the other. It is messy, but then he was disagreeing with Dad. Sara and Dad keep up eye contact and a softly enunciated conversation between them starts. Unconsciously maybe, Dad deploys Sara's presence in a series of well-tried strategies.

One is Sara diplomatically diverting attention: 'Sorry, I didn't hear what you said – would you mind saying it again?' Dad gets more time to think things through and the visitor's negotiating strategy is thrown off balance. Interrupting visitor's speech with phrases like 'Oh my cat, yes, you, my cat ...' excuses lack of attention as the presentation is bought to a crescendo. Effect: visitor blinks and concludes Dad must be either harmless or so eccentric that he is in effect harmless. Visitor thrown off guard and badly misled. Worse, Dad continues talking to cat but in a much louder voice and goes into details about the feline life ('Did the naughty bird fly away?' and other such nonsense) until visitor has nearly finished his speech when Dad turns around and apologises: 'I'm not sure we understood what you said.' Visitor panics. Does the 'we' refer to the cat? What bit isn't understood by which one – him or the cat? Do I have to repeat the proposition? Is this bloke eccentric? Oh gee, what do I do here? At which point, perfectly understood by Sara, Dad reveals his real agenda. Visitor splutters in his teacup; Dad's attention reverts to Sara.

A variation is feeding the cat bits from the refreshments. The visitor is saying 'I don't think a 7.5 per cent royalty on the Japanese edition is generous enough. I am earning more in other countries.'

'What's that got to do with it?' asks Dad.

'Well I don't see why I should have to earn less from Japan.'

'Oh yes, you like that don't you?'

'Pardon?'

'I was talking to the cat. She likes that. So we'll settle on 7.5 per cent, shall we? ... Oh Sara, you're greedy.'

It usually works, but if needed there are tougher options. If the visitor gets wound up, unleashing his body language, Sara suddenly launches herself. There she is sitting on him, purring. It normally calms the visitor; certainly roots him to the spot.

Of course, Sara can pretend to like the visitor. Her not inconsiderable charms – purring, wriggling and generally squirming about – undo anyone's concentration. Should the visitor get heated up again over irrelevant matters such as money and wave their arms around, Sara treats it as a game. The arms need to be batted down. Visitor immobilised and silenced.

The final battle scenario is the one Sara most enjoys. Its fundamental principle is not to let the visitor say anything at all. Many of these visitors come vast distances, sometimes across oceans and they can scarcely go home to their bosses and say they met Dad but didn't say anything. So agreement is always assumed. The guided tour makes a perfect camouflage. Dad says, 'So you have to be on the 9.30 train, which means you will need to leave here by nine and it's now just gone seven so we have time for a walk.'

Everyone piles out of the lounge, sister's door bangs again, and Dad and visitor and Sara set off.

After about half an hour visitor attempts to start talking business. Sara understands that Dad isn't ready so, to buy time, she runs up a tree and pretends she can't come down. This leads to lots of apologies and rushing around finding ladders. If that tactic is working really well and it's getting dark, torches are brought out ... but need new batteries. Train times are again cited; unfortunately there never is a later one.

Dancing is another of Sara's distractions. In spring she likes to partner with a bed of daffodils. Even hardened businessmen can't ignore the sight of her lovely white-and-black-pointed Siamese features constantly weaving through a yellow bed as if she herself were the revolving wind. One way or another, these walks always take up longer than expected which, along with food and drink, leaves only a few moments for business. With Sara's help, Dad is quite capable of filling all that himself.

There's worse: a tried and tested ancient technique. Scare them speechless. Sensing this is called for, Sara demands to be let out, soon reappearing with a large dead animal generously deposited at the visitor's feet. Rumpus follows; people rush hither and thither with trowels and cloths. Ignoring the hubbub, Sara keeps her eyes firmly on the visitor and stretches. And stretches and stretches ... making herself look even longer by showing claws and stretching yet further. Then she releases just half a yelp. (Her full yelp would have curdled the blood of a banshee.) Result: visitor goes quiet. Sara reinforces the silence by jumping on visitor's lap without purr.

It was only last year in one of the vast halls of the Frankfurt Book Fair that a rare species indeed mentioned David's cat. He was a brilliantly successful American publisher, who has kept his job for over twenty years. He asked after my dad and asked, 'Does he still have that cat?' I told him there were two now and he groaned. I understand Dad met with him recently and I think I know how it went.

CORONA

Chapter 7

AFTER SARA

One of the privileges of being a writer is that some of your readers tell you about their own comparable experiences in a way they would not generally feel free to do. Together with kind comments on my obituary of Sara came accounts of the way in which other cats had ended their lives, along with those of how the joy of existence had enabled them to overcome earlier health problems or accidents. Cats are better patients than is sometimes realised, but once teeth start decaying, or some disability sets in, or bones simply become stiffer with age, it is a steadily downhill process for many. Naturally the real drama is usually right at the end.

In the majority of the cases reported, the cat somehow behaved well even in dying, gently making the most of its last days, hanging onto life until the return of its owner or for some other special reason, accepting what was to be with quiet dignity, usually accompanied by purring – albeit feeble – until the last hour. While a few cats, such as a friend's Drifter – so called because he simply drifted into her life – give companionship for many years but ultimately slip away to die in solitude, most rely increasingly on human support at their life's end. What is very awkward is when the final decline coincides with something of such importance that the owner has to be elsewhere.

Another friend and writer was deeply upset when her lilac-point Gemma was in obvious decline just as she had to go to Japan for her son's marriage to a local girl there. That Gemma had been a fine cat is confirmed by her featuring in many advertisements of feline products. She really took to the camera, and was well paid in kind: food, litter, cat toys and baskets. She was a clever cat, routinely able to open window latches, and much set in her routine: up at seven sharp, an inspection of her territory including a terrifying (for her owner) trip to the roof, a nap and then a long semi-somnolent period under the desk while her owner wrote on her computer. Ten o'clock, almost to the minute, was her bedtime; the owner knew exactly how late it was without having to look at a clock. Aged twelve, Gemma lost her sight but, after a few bumps into furniture, quickly adapted, always walking round the edge of a room to the door. Two years later she went deaf, but still coped well and indeed ruled the household including the smaller Burmese, Bronte, whom she still washed. Gemma had always been obsessed with cleanliness.

We can imagine the sorrow when her owner said what she thought would be her final farewell, as she left Gemma at a cattery to fly off to her son's wedding. Gemma, however, had other ideas. Though obviously struggling, she was still alive when her owner returned home. Then she even did what she usually did on coming back from the cattery: ate a large meal. It was to be her last, for after eating it she went to bed and stayed there for three days, occasionally raising her head and staring blindly into space as if she was aware that someone was close by. Her owner stroked her, which was obviously welcome, though Gemma couldn't hear what was being said to her. On the last day her breathing was shallower and, with that extra sense we know cats have but don't yet understand, became agitated if the one she loved left the room. Says her owner: 'So I stayed beside her, just sitting quietly and stroking her as she slipped away. It was as though she had held on to die with me comforting her — or was it for my benefit?'

Other readers reported similar experiences, one of a cat hanging on until her husband returned from a business trip 'so we'd all be together'. Several readers movingly described how they stroked their cats while the vet put them peacefully to sleep.

Chocolate-point Cleo and lilac-point Cassie were sisters. I met them in the Mitre Bookshop in Newton Abbot, Devon, when they were little more than kittens, and then not again until they were in old age though still always graciously curious and free with their purr. Cleo had to be put to sleep with failing kidneys, aged eighteen. 'I held her paw and stroked her as she went,' said the owner. After that, I met Cassie several times: feeble, unable to jump onto my lap but still anxious to come for a gentle stroke. She was very thin, clearly nearing her end, yet one didn't at all need to pity her. She was still her own person, keeping an eye on what was happening and welcoming visitors allowed in the private quarters above the shop. Her owner said, 'She was a great friend. She died peacefully of a heart attack when she was nineteen. Such a treasure.'

At which point I have to declare that the one thing I deeply regret about Sara is that, overcome by emotion, I was a coward leaving her to be collected by the vet. I should have been there to stroke her as she ceased to be. I think perhaps I feared that the vet who had been terrorised by her might say something inappropriate.

The decision to end her life was, however, right. Though a less apt description of vociferous Sara than 'a dumb animal' would be hard to find, she couldn't understand or comment as she lost her dignity with her rapidly deteriorating kidneys. After the experience with the family cats of my boyhood, I had vowed never to terminate a pet's life artificially, but the decision to bring in the vet was surely in keeping with the brief Sara had seemed to give me on the evening I fetched her to live with me: 'You are mine. I belong to you which gives you great responsibility.' But, oh, I wish I had been there to hold her and talk to her; her hearing was still acutely sharp.

There are several reasons why I didn't think it sensible to replace her quickly. Perhaps the main one was that she was still very much with me; she had become and to this day remains a vital part of my being. Of course I missed her, curiously perhaps most of all her gently flipping her velvety ears when my face was close to her and she was listening hard to what I was whispering. But I knew that no other cat, whatever pleasures it inspired, could be the same, any more than a human who has lost a spouse can remarry anyone of the same ilk.

Incidentally, even had it been possible at an affordable price, I would never consider cloning, for which a few kitten owners have now paid huge sums. I detest the increasing element of design in cats, occasionally leading to disastrous consequences. A publishing friend told me of his sad experience with a Siamese that began as the sweetest of kittens and then steadily regarded him and his wife as enemies viciously to attack. 'The vet said it was due to over-inbreeding and could only get worse, so sadly we had to put it down. Apparently it happens occasionally, though not with the best of breeders. We made a mistake where we went to buy the kitten.'

I never thought of erecting a memorial to Sara, let alone one as expensive as the Christian cross commemorating the life of a favourite cat in 900AD. It was recently sold for over £20,000 at Sotheby's, though we can only guess what it cost in its day. My extensive library of memories, supplemented by photographs and writings, has been more than enough to keep her alive in me.

Another reason for not replacing her was that I spent an increasing amount of time travelling, at first largely for business and then mainly for pleasure, including many trips lecturing on the *QE2*. I had reached the stage of needing to unwind and read for enjoyment – not possible on office days when faced with the slush heap of unsolicited manuscripts. Sara herself hated the manuscripts and the concentration I had to give to turning the pages rapidly in order to judge which were worth more detailed study. I used to read them lying in bed and often threw one to be rejected to the floor, where Sara would patiently wait to jump onto me as I finished turning the sheets of that evening's last submission. Reviewing the slush heap was emptier and more depressing during the few years I continued to do it after she had gone.

So it was a long decade and a half before there was again a cat to greet my homecoming. It was during this interlude (virtually a healthy cat's lifespan) that I finally and fully became a cat person. I went out of my way to meet them, talk about them and read what other people had to say about them. Especially in the period immediately after Sara's death, I published books about them, some with my own words included. I went to more cat shows, worked with cat charities, revelled in the cats I really got to know in relatives' homes, and enjoyed more casual encounters on my walks, often renewing friendships with one or more cats on my rounds. And though I was without one myself, cat ownership flourished among the staff. At one time we counted well over a hundred 'office' cats, of many hues and idiosyncrasies.

I learned much about them: for instance, cats have 250 bones compared with the 206 in humans, the difference roughly accounted for by those in their unique tails, so much more sophisticated than the tails of lions, tigers and the other large wild cats. And I learned much from them, particularly that most business is only a glorified game, and that cats generally have a more wholesome lifestyle, closer to the world that God gave us and with fewer psychological hiccups and long-term anxieties. Think about it: at least for cats with good homes, there is a life of contentment with no worries about mortgage or pension, promotion or losing a job, or even status in a club or society. No wonder greeting card manufacturers so frequently deploy them to signify bliss. Again and again, I noticed how often people compared a cat's life enviously with their own, and how those with cats were generally less uptight than those without pets. What goes for cats is probably also substantially true for dogs, but I met more cat people and we published more books about cats than dogs. However, there is one significant difference between cat and dog owners. A cat lover will proudly show pictures of their 'unique' feline, proclaiming, 'He is my boss' or 'She rules my life'. This is in sharp contrast with dog lovers who tell their buddies how obedient their pets are.

I found this observation useful when it came to working with cat-owning authors. The best way to slow down Patrick (later Sir Patrick) Moore when he rattled off thoughts and decisions faster than you could digest them was suddenly to ask him how his cat of the moment was doing. Patrick veritably purred himself as he told how she welcomed him when he returned late from a television studio and how they relaxed together at bedtime. Patrick, predictably just like most people talking about their cat, speaks as though his is in a class of her own. I used to think it was standard boasting, similar to 'My runner beans are longer than yours.' But cats are utterly individual in their habits of endearment, and often so besotted with their owners and, when not sleeping, devoting everything they have to increasing their repertoire of curious behaviour, that many justify the use of the word 'unique'.

Authors of books about cats themselves were invariably friendly and co-operative if sometimes eccentric. It used to be said in the office that they were not the best organised and were generally pretty weak on basic maths – such as ten times a thousand words makes 10,000 words – but they didn't bargain unreasonably. When I complained to Patrick Moore that I found his agent a bit of a tyrant, he walked over to my typewriter and, without warning, wrote a letter sacking him. In their relaxed way, cat authors weren't afraid that you would do them down. Sharing a love of cats made author and publisher trust one another – a tall but accurate claim. Moreover, while most authors insisted on putting themselves in the foreground with 'I' this and 'I' that, those who wrote about cats were happy to let them be the hero. My top managers undoubtedly thought my cat enthusiasm went over the top, but agreed it was harmless and the books sold.

A favourite has always been *John Gay's Book of Cats*. One of the last monochrome albums before colour became all conquering, it lovingly portrays real cats whose personalities you can quickly comprehend in all kinds of true-to-life poses. Most of today's bargain cat albums are nothing like as satisfying. John asked me to write an introduction, which explained how he approached cat photography:

> *John Gay spends time getting to know the cat or, more important, letting the cat get to know him. 'The cat has to make the first move.' He waits patiently while the cat explores natural and sometimes unnatural surroundings so that eventually he can capture an expression or antic that is characteristic and so easily recognisable by those with a cat of the same kind in the family.*

As one might perhaps expect, John had strong personal preferences. 'Give me an alley cat every time,' he said. But though the aristocratic pure breeds might generally be less rewarding to work with, some have their place in his book, and indeed one of John Gay's 'clients' was in its day the most famous cat in the advertising world.

The most ambitious of the cat titles has already been mentioned: *A Passion for Cats*, in which we brought together a magnificent range of colour and monochrome photographs (including a handsome tabby lying on a path with the caption 'If you could walk past without saying hello, you shouldn't be reading this book!'), creative writing by real cat lovers, practical advice and good fun. Published in association with what is now Cats Protection, it raised their profile as well as substantial royalties. Unusually it has two forewords.

In his, Desmond Morris talks about the contract man made with the cat 4000 years ago:

> *You help us and we will look after you; you protect our food stores from mice and rats and we will care for you and protect you. This was a fair contract and both sides benefited. Out of it grew the domestic cat, more friendly, more kittenish than its wild ancestors and a valued servant in the home. Those ancient cats were revered … Then came the Dark Ages and the cat suffered centuries of torment at the hands of pious witch-hunters who stupidly labelled it as one of Satan's helpers. Only in recent times has the cat once again become a much loved companion animal in our homes. But even now it is maltreated by a cruel minority and all too often turned out to fend for itself. It is resilient and it somehow manages to scrape a living, but that is not good enough for so magnificent an animal.*

In her foreword, Beryl Reid cheekily says that when she told her agent she intended writing *The Cat's Whiskers*, he replied that it was a good idea since more people liked cats than her. She concluded he was right and the book was a great success. Writing with Jenny sitting on the television, Dimley straight in front of her and Cleopatra 'seeing to some extraordinary parts of her anatomy, making sure they're awfully clean', she tells that cats are …

> *extremely good for anyone who is excitable or who has heart trouble or high blood pressure. If you live with cats, those are non-existent. They all have their extraordinary ways of eating, as we know: Patrick (named after Patrick Cargill), who, when he was alive, was King Cat or Leader of the Pack, had a passion for taking roses out of a vase and eating them. Or cabbage stalks – it was like Cabbages and Kings, really. They are wonderfully soothing to be with, and they're very very restful. I'm so glad to know that people like Churchill must have got great satisfaction from the cats who reigned with him in Downing Street – Nelson, Margate and Jock – and that the cat who has just died, Wilberforce, who served under four prime ministers, had special perks – the police were instructed to ring the front door bell any time he made it known that he wished to enter.*

Though carefully edited into a smoothly rounded whole by cat lovers in the office – it was great fun, I recall – *A Passion for Cats* had many contributors who gave their time and enthusiasm free. Rereading it the other day, I was especially taken by the extract on 'Church Cats' from Francis Hunter's *Cats* which was among many other titles we published:

The cats participated fully in the life of the church. At a baptism they would move among the people, giving particular pleasure to the children. At weddings, Thomas Aquinas had a way of sidling between the bride-to-be and her father as they went up the aisle. Then the two cats would slip away and appear again outside on the pavement among the guests, when the bride and bridegroom were getting into their car. Over the Christmas period they sat in the crib, in the hay, eyes glinting. A child was heard to exclaim: 'Why! they're real animals!' For days the cats' fur smelt of hay. Parishioners brought them Christmas gifts: packets of cat's food — even a small roast chicken!

Finally from *A Passion for Cats*, a few of the comments from a section headed 'Writers' Cats':

You can't look at a sleeping cat and feel tense.
Jane Pauley

There is, indeed, no single quality of the cat that man could not emulate to his advantage.
Carl Van Vechten

Cats seem to go on the principle that it never does any harm to ask what you want.
Joseph Wood Krutch

Even in Europe the cat's cry is 'meow'.
Ceylonese proverb

Cats know how to obtain food without labour, shelter without confinement, and love without penalties.
Walter Lionel George

Only once was there a cat in the office. His arrival caused more of a stir than that of famous people such as the Archbishop of Canterbury. The phone kept ringing.

'He just walked in, Mr Thomas.'

'We've given him some milk.'

'What *will* we do, Mr Thomas?'

'He's so sweet, you can't possibly send him away.'

Nothing would have delighted me more than an office cat, but with a busy five-track railway to one side and roads on the other three, one of them a trunk route, there would have been scant chance of survival. 'He could be an indoor cat, Mr Thomas.' Not in an office used by hundreds of people, by no means all cat-loving careful door-closers. 'At least we can keep him tonight. I'll buy some food during my lunch break.'

Not since a dozen burley policemen had followed me at high speed from office to office (I agreed generously to support their charitable effort if they joined me in acting the fool and stirring up the staff) had there been such tension and ringing of internal phones. Anything out of the ordinary – 'managing by surprise' one director called it – was good for productivity, which no doubt dropped the next day when the owner of the adorable black-and-white kitten, with a black head and dainty white patch just reaching to his nose, discovered where his pet was and came to claim him. His whereabouts had been revealed in pub talk.

Lacking my own cat certainly didn't leave me totally bereft. The most loved cats in my life were those of my former wife. I regularly visited her parents; the cats were always with them in the largest and warmest room in the house … a room, moreover, nearly always with people and welcoming laps and so perfect for the pair of Burmese boys. Their peculiarity was jumping on top of the grandfather clock every time the crunching of the works said it was on the hour. The actual bell had gone wrong but, at the first sound of the deep-throated mechanism getting underway, they competed for the uppermost perch and wondered at the mystery of the muffled cranking, descending a minute or so after the hourly performance had finished. They never seemed to tire of the ritual.

The smaller, more athletic and outgoing of the pair was brown Brandy who I taught to revel in being thrown a yard or so onto a couch. The first time in each session, he looked slightly puzzled and took a moment or two to regain his senses. Then, with bent-back tail and quivering hind, he'd present himself for more, purring in expectation of his next short flight. As with many Orientals, a sharp spank just in front of his tail sent him into ecstasy, slobbering, rubbing himself against me and doing his special pianissimo chirruping. Then he'd settle down on my lap until it was again on the hour when he'd race his brother up the grandfather clock. Brandy was great fun, and over the years grew steadily more excited when he saw me arriving. I enjoyed him during visits at least once a week for many years.

Soda, a large handsome fawn animal, might have been the larger of the two but always seemed a bit of an afterthought … like soda water added to the brandy. In fact, he was very loving in a gentler way. As I recall, even his purr was more subtle. Possibly he would have been happier as an only cat. But for a reason that still makes me squirm, he was to go.

I used to take my ex-parents-in-law out; we had become close, and they could no longer drive. After tea at a café on Dartmoor one evening, I was taking them home in the autumn gloaming when, between the granite gateposts at the entrance to a drive serving several houses including theirs, I felt a bump. I stopped and looked around, but couldn't see or hear anything. When my former wife came to the door to meet her mum and dad, I mentioned it to her. 'Oh dear,' she said. 'Soda has been out for ages and he will sometimes sit in the road.'

She went out to look and came back with bad news. Soda was quickly taken to the vet, but there was nothing that could be done. What could be worse for a cat lover than to kill his former wife's cat with her parents on board? They were all sympathetic, treating me as though I were the injured one; I was indeed in shock, as would be any cat lover with similar misfortune.

It was as though Brandy became stronger stuff without the Soda. Each visit we continued just where we had left off. I heard much about him, including how at 12.45 on a Sunday he had been discovered bringing a whole chicken into the kitchen. A quick ring round neighbours failed to reveal who had lost their Sunday lunch, so we can only imagine what the losers thought when they couldn't find their bird.

Talking about food, it strikes me that in all the time I knew Brandy and Soda, I never fed them a morsel. Cats let the appropriate person know when they need, *instantly* need, feeding, but eating is a matter quite separate from the rest of life. With most cats it has little or nothing to do with love, friendship or play. They are perhaps the least food orientated of mammals.

Eventually, of course, Brandy died, as did my former father-in-law whom I still called Grandad. Years later, Granny went into an old people's home and suffered a stroke. I spent hours quietly talking to her, receiving only one reaction during what must have been several years of visits. This is a dog matter rather than a cat one, but emphasises the role that pets play. One visit I recalled aloud her former dog, Tuffy, and his antics. She smiled and uttered the one word I believe anyone heard her say after her stroke: 'Tuffy'.

With memories of the encounter with the naughty Burmese who interfered with our game of croquet at the Worcestershire hotel when she was a girl, my daughter Alyss has favoured this breed. First on the scene was Tulip, a spirited but always gentle grey Burmese. When Alyss was living alone and went away, it fell to me to unlock her ground-floor flat and call Tulip. Usually she raced in within seconds, hungry for food but even more so for human contact and love.

I watched her cope with the dilemma of whether to snatch more love while it was available or assuage her hunger. Her tail switched forth and back (usually a sign of an undecided cat rather than the popular belief that tail waving denotes anger) as she eyed my lap and the food bowl. The food bowl was empty, everything left on my previous visit having been eaten. Usually it was only when I stood up that she became desperate about the food … and then not so much to eat right away but more to make sure I didn't depart without her sniffing and checking again that her next meal was being left. I have known many cats far more worried that they might not be left food than anxious to eat it immediately or indeed in the next hour.

At the time of writing Tulip is a fulfilled fifteen, less active but still very much part of life and always ready to make the best of whatever the current situation; recently she has had to share life in the home of another cat lover.

Truffle, a sleek chocolate Burmese, followed two years later. Always more excitable and demanding, he must have spent an aggregate of several years wailing at the top of his voice, often running upstairs and down to make sure everyone knew he was in need of greater attention. Recently he has been seriously put out sharing a house with other cats ... and not very nice to one of them either. He would probably have been an adorable pet but for his early upbringing.

Here is an example of a cat who was to have been kept by the breeder for stud but was sold after a change of mind. Insufficient time must have been devoted to handling him and developing his social skills in those vital early weeks. 'I wouldn't make that mistake again, and we should warn others to avoid it,' says Alyss. The experience seems to have damaged her basic enthusiasm for cats. 'They only think of themselves,' she said in a desperate moment the other day when Truffle was misbehaving and complaining simultaneously.

But perhaps all is not lost. On the telephone recently I heard a delighted eighteen-month-old grandson chortle away. Yes, said his mum: 'He's playing with Truffle who loves him even if he pulls his tail; Truffle is ever so gentle with him.' Another cat victory?

Meanwhile, 12,000 miles away in New Zealand, my son also had a Burmese (brown with white undercarriage and black toes 'which he didn't quite believe and admired intently'). Gareth had gone to an animal shelter 'just to think about getting a cat' and – surprise – returned with the twelve-week-old Bandicoot for no better reason than 'he came up and attacked me in fun, wanting us to get connected'. I met him happily growing up in his new home, a house surrounded by woodland on a cliff at Titirangi, Auckland. Bandicoot was always playful and helped give balance to Gareth's somewhat work-obsessed life. As Gareth described it: ' "You've done enough of that," he would intimate, jumping up and down on the desk – or on the printer when it was printing – leading me out of the office and into the garden to play together.'

A second kitten came from the same animal shelter: Coriander, a dumb blonde, affectionate to those she really knew but superiorly wary of strangers, and who became increasingly assertive as she grew older. She became definite boss of the two cats who belonged to someone else who came to live with Gareth. Dumb blonde she may have been, but she knew not only how to remain the dominant cat but – especially when she 'had that certain look' – how to increase her share of being stroked, and expected it to be her turn even when Bandicoot had fussily rushed in for attention first.

For a time there was a fifth cat, driven in almost as it were on the wings of a big storm. He instantly settled into living as part of the family but, two years later, when there was another huge storm, he took it as a signal to move on again.

There were rats on the beach, which both Bandicoot and Coriander hunted. Making a 'presentation', once Coriander released a rat too soon, and it ran back down to the beach – to be re-caught by Bandicoot. Later on, however, aged nine, Bandicoot lost his life as the result of being bitten by a rat and the housesitter not arranging treatment soon enough. Gareth was working in New York when told the news: 'I still miss him and his special ways.'

Now aged twelve, Coriander flourishes but stayed with the house when Gareth moved to Australia's rural New South Wales, where there are too many snakes, spiders and other risks for it to be safe for a cat. I've no doubt cats will reappear in his later life.

The New Zealand homes of other publishers also offered encounters with friendly cats: I especially recall a Burmese boy who assumed I had come halfway round the world specifically to befriend him. In Australia, the most colourful cat memory is of being at a publishers' barbecue where I was being introduced to the local guests when a black moggie strode in, tail and voice both up, and walked in front of the next person whose hand I was about to shake. Luckily this guest was a cat lover, too; only the host thought that (as an Englishman, or Pom) I might be offended. That I spent part of the party with the cat on my lap no doubt contributed to the flattering statement toward the event's end that I wasn't 'an ordinary Pom at all'. It was also in Australia where a small-scale publisher, who said she had been nervous of meeting me, found me talking to a cat and said, 'That's all right then. If you like cats, you won't be difficult to get on with.' To give a fair balance, it has to be said that there were also those in whose estimation one's reputation collapsed for being peculiar in talking to a cat.

It was only in New Zealand and Australia — exciting countries in which to do business — that cats played such a role for, with the exception of beloved Ying at the rural

HQ of our little American branch in Vermont, American business in later years meant skyscraper offices, martini lunches and parties at which no self-respecting feline would have lingered even if invited. There were to be no more visits to private homes with cats, though there were some pretty odd ones where a moggie would surely have brought a touch of normality. Come to think of it, one of the few things I regret having said about cats was when I stormed out of a New York publisher who was obviously trying to cheat me. 'You people have the morality of a cat,' I shouted, leaving the room and banging the door. Why I chose to abuse cats I cannot imagine. I never saw the publisher's reaction or had further contact. But after all these years: 'Sorry, cats.'

Back to the Southern Hemisphere, where the only examples I have heard of cats receiving the kiss of life come, one each, from New Zealand and Australia. Both involved house fires and firemen acting heroically. However, not all of hot Australia is cat heaven and, naturally, there were no cats on board a special carriage attached to the country's famous outback train, the *Ghan*, which we rented for ourselves, Gareth, his wife Benny, and a school friend of well over half a century ago and her husband. A less congenial countryside for cats one could hardly imagine. But on the fabulous journey from Alice Springs to Adelaide, Margaret Woods was, shall we say, full of her cats with complicated names and lifestyles. As a glimpse of the international correspondence that cats engender, here is Margaret's list of recent felines:

The Late Catpain Merlin, a traditional tabby, (26 October 1985–30 April 1991) was the adored son of Mrs Milo Woods, Widow of Independent Means, (russet double tabby 20 April 1985–18 February 2003) and an Unknown Father reputed to be a Made Cat of the local PAWFIA (Wallaroo Chapter) [for the uninitiated, the cats' mafia]. Engaged to the haughty Abyssinian Miss Zula Plummer of Huntsworth Meows, Regents Park, and Limpley Stoke, Bath, theirs was a star-crossed romance. The Late Catpain Merlin spent many years saving up to travel to London where he knew the streets were paved with gold. He had a red spotted hankie given as a token of her affection by Miss Zula Plummer, but she kept getting engaged to other toms and Catpain Merlin never saw England.

Like his dear mother, he held the local PAWFIA franchise for Driede Mise and managed the Wallaroo Home for Fallen Pussies. He died on duty as guard cat. He was bitten by a redback spider. He was buried with full honours on the property, wrapped in his red spotted hankie.

On 17 June 1986 the Russian Blue Morgan le Fay arrived, age unknown, being rescued from a locally rented house after the tenants had fled owing rent. She died tragically after being shot by local (twelve-year-old) thugs two years later.

Mordred, a non-descript grey fluffo, aged about five weeks, was abandoned by children to whom she had been given as a yuletide gift, in December 1986. She was tossed over the local library fence and suffered broken bones and internal injuries. Her story was told in a heartrending letter in the South Australian Advertiser. After a short tragic life, Mordred was put peacefully to sleep aged only two when ongoing health problems destroyed any quality of life.

On 17 April 1987 Miss Mallory a tortie Burmese joined the family at six months old. She, too, led a blameless but spirited and happy life inspired by the example of The Late Catpain Merlin. She died of old age in 2002.

Found rooting through the family dustbin, the long-haired black Morgan arrived on 1 September 1993, aged about one. Morgan had been abandoned by a holidaying family and was evidently starving. Morgan is highly socialised and must once have had a loving home. A very rewarding cat, he has replaced the much loved Late Catpain Merlin as senior guard and family support cat. Morgan and the bereaved Mrs Milo Woods became great friends. The family moved to a farm in 1998. Morgan now supplemented the family larder with rabbits (up to eight in a week) snakes, mice and rats. Mrs Milo Woods died peacefully of old age whilst admiring her 18th birthday present of a clockwork hedgehog.

On 27 February 2003 the family acquired Misty, aged four, from the SA Animal Welfare League in Adelaide. Alas Misty, too, had been an abused cat and was unable to trust humans or Morgan who had hoped to have a friend to replace the beloved Mrs Milo Woods. Misty, possibly as result of earlier mistreatment, died suddenly of liver failure only eight weeks later. Morgan was again alone.

A lifelong dream was fulfilled in 2003 when the opportunity arose to acquire two pedigree British Shorthair Blue ladies, surplus to a cattery's requirements. Molly, at three, had not grown to full size and was, and is, still only the size of a three-month kitten. Mathilda, named appropriately after an old British Queen, was eight. Molly and Mathilda, with their thick plush fur, big orange eyes and sweet faces look exactly like cuddly toys. Molly and Mathilda (known to her many friends as Matey) provide Morgan at long last with affectionate and loyal friends to replace the Late beloved Mrs Milo Woods, Widow of Independent Means. And Morgan has, in his own kindly fashion, largely succeeded in dulling the pain of the loss of the Late Catpain Merlin. So the story ends happily.

Just one of dozens of letters about people's cats received during the writing of this book. Cats surely have more written about them in letters, books and newspapers than all other pets together. They are also the subject of an astonishing range of legends from around the world. Though many are about good and bad luck, there is great variety, including cats' involvement with human souls. Thus in ancient Thailand it was said that when a holy person died their soul entered a cat and ascended to heaven only when the cat reached the end of its life. Two cats fighting around a dying person or their grave represented an angel and the devil fighting for the soul's possession.

Manx cats lost their tail when they were the last creatures to board Noah's ark and the door closed on them. My favourite legend with a religious background says that Mary was so grateful to a tabby for purring Jesus to sleep in the manger that she rewarded all tabbies with a letter M on their foreheads. The first tabby I saw last Christmas certainly displayed one.

However, while there were still many cats in my life, I frequently felt bereft without my own and scarcely a day passed during which Sara did not drift into my mind. She had indeed become part of my personality, and continued to appear in some of the publicity material for my new books. After a time, I did not so much mourn her as give praise for her memory and what she did for me.

Chapter 8

BEFORE THE NEWCOMERS

As I steadily became more of a cat person, correspondence telling of owners' individual ones and the extraordinary role they played in family life enlivened many a breakfast time. Sometimes it was just a line on a Christmas card, or a PS to an ordinary letter, but increasingly people wrote specially about their cats, which gave much comfort while I was still without one of my own, now living beside the Moray Firth in Scotland.

Occasionally cat information told my wife and I about a person's character. For example, a correspondent said she was temporarily away 'baby sitting' the cat of an enthusiastic owner who was about to move to our town. We astonished the newcomer when we first met her by asking how Percy had coped during her recent holiday. We still receive regular bulletins, keeping tabs on Percy — as we do on dozens of other cats — as the owner and he have steadily moved around Britain. I may never see Percy, but to me he is very real.

For keeping me fully informed on the cat front, only slightly behind Margaret Woods, the Australian writer of the final quote in the last chapter, is the English naturalist Trevor Beer. Extracts from recent letters tell their own story.

I was down in the garden checking a large aquarium in which I kept palmate newts, to study. It was early morning and I bent down to look into the tank and was startled to see a face staring into mine. Crouched behind the aquarium watching me through the glass was a tabby. I called and out it came, wet in the misty rain, straight into my arms. Indoors, dried and fluffy it (she) ate and settled down. We called her Misty and she'd sleep across my shoulders when I was in an armchair. She was not young but we had some good years together before she passed on.

Shortly after, I went into the porch to look out at the pouring rain one evening. A tabby was crouched by the porch door, soaked through. I picked it up and cuddled it, took it indoors, towelled it and it stayed. It was a male tabby with white paws. Jasper I named him and he was with us for years until he died last year. Whilst he was with us another tabby, from along the avenue, often came to sit with him in the sun on the flat roof of top-shed.

When Jasper passed on we lost sight of the other cat for a couple or three weeks. Then one day there he was at our back door. His 'owners' were having an extension built so we thought he was fed up with the noise. But no, that was over a year ago and Rascal is still here, content. He has his favourite spots as all cats do and still loves top-shed roof. His previous 'owners' didn't even come looking for him and so Rascal has made his decision. It must be my beard they like.

This very morning I went along the lane behind our place, which immediately adjoins woodland, as I could hear a Greater Spotted Woodpecker drumming and wanted to see it. Rascal came too but when he reached the boundary fence of his former home he stopped, then ran home to our gate, to wait for me. He is very territorial and chins everything, bushes, trees, pots in the garden. A fine cat.

Once again we have been adopted ... by yet another tabby, an oldish one I feel, with white paws. I'll say her because I think she is a lady. She was sitting in the middle of the avenue next to ours with what can only be called a death wish. The traffic veered slightly one way or the other to avoid her. No one else stopped, so we have her here. She took food and milk and is now curled up on a chair beside me. It took hours for her to relax and close her eyes, but I have told her she has no worries and is loved. Rascal (who is still very much with us) climbed up, sniffed her and strolled off as though a stranger had been expected. She is old and dehydrated, I can feel her backbone and she is wobbly, maybe on her last legs. But she must have been someone's cat. I fear she has been tossed out ...

Whoops! She has just gotten up and gone out for a while, I must follow her ... Now she is back. She wobbled around the garden, then came in and settled on a cushion. Strange but lovely animals. I have named her Spring, cos it is April and there's hope. Shades of Misty.

On reading and hearing about cats, the thing which always comes across is their sheer adaptability. They may all be hunters by nature, and they may have their favourite places to sleep and their own kind of exceptional behaviour; but they are equally successful in being what they are, enjoying life, needing human company, showing love, and courage when need be, in an enormous range of habitats.

From urban slums to palatial rural mansions, homes of all sizes and characters are colonised by cats — whether or not the occupants actually choose to have one. Cats have lived side by side at times of vital importance with many presidents and prime ministers. They have settled comfortably and have themselves become showpieces in the great houses of yesteryear now maintained by the National Trust in the UK and its opposite numbers around the Western world.

With the decline in industry and the merger of small farms into larger ones, the number of working cats has naturally declined, but where there is a vacancy it is quickly and diligently filled. In Britain, from the Home Office and other government departments and from post offices to the railways, cats have often appeared on the payroll; that is to say an allowance has been authorised for their food and care.

On railway stations, as on sailing and small cargo ships, and in many offices and private hotels, in the homes of priests and occasionally even in their churches, the cat is often the best-known and remembered figure. Seriously, I cannot recall the name of a single member of staff at a luxury hotel on Dartmoor, but Wally the Siamese, who always gave the impression he ran the show, is firmly and fondly recalled, I am sure, by hundreds. It is the popularity of cats that comes across in many letters and reports.

Harry, who was found curled up in the carpenter's tool kit before being taken on board, was probably the most popular living thing on Shackleton's *Endurance*. Much was the relief when, after he had fallen into the polar waters, the ship turned round and he was fished out in a net, none the worse ... a phrase that repeatedly occurs in accounts of cats' lives. And much was the upset when Shackleton ordered Harry's shooting as, trapped in Antarctic ice, the ship began to break up and had to be abandoned. Cats might then have been taken for granted on land, but at sea they always played a special role. Centuries later, in Wellington, New Zealand, perhaps Harry has the last laugh, for many stop to admire his bronze re-creation, which incidentally scares a few dogs when they suddenly find themselves faced by a cat.

Tiddles, the famous Paddington station cat, showed how things should be organised. His career began humbly in the ladies loo but steadily stretched to greeting passengers – including VIPs – on the platform, and receiving admirers. From the start, he made it plain he wasn't a common working cat but needed his own fridge, stocked with steak, liver and chicken. Even some hospitals, along with schools and colleges, have their resident cat, again frequently one of the best-known personalities around.

An empty building, or even a vacant piece of urban land, is quickly colonised by cats, while out in the country there have always been felines specialising in riverside life. Those I have seen have been more intent on hunting the wildlife along the banks than getting their paws wet, but fishing cats are well recorded. One family wondered how their large tabby sustained himself when seemingly he ate so little. Apparently he did consume some food at home just to show gratitude. What he really liked was trout, one of which he daily caught himself. This became clear when his owner stumbled on a heap of trout bones, some of which were not wholly devoid of flesh since the cat preferred fresh trout, and some he caught were too large for a single day's consumption.

Is it surprising that humans find it so difficult to give cats the food they desire when in the wild they choose such different diets? In bygone days, many cats lost their lives — or at least a paw — in mantraps used by farmers to keep off marauders who might upset the precious pheasant shooting. Long after mantraps were officially banned around the end of the first third of the nineteenth century, their use remained common ... and most gamekeepers regarded cats as their enemy. Though few cats took pheasants, the other valued wild creature, the rabbit, was much to the taste of many. Some would eat nothing else.

In the days of near-starvation pay for farm workers, the occasional poached rabbit obviously made a huge difference, but poaching was a dangerous business, possibly carrying the death penalty. So what joy when the family cat did it for them! Their cat's gift was usually deposited somewhat short of its intended destination — cats still tend to do that — so that occasionally a rabbit would make its escape before the eyes of the hungry owner. Sometimes a rabbit might be re-caught, but a hare — which would have been a particular treat — was more likely to dash off at high speed. Bitter disappointment for cat and owner.

Other cats have been known to concentrate on eating other single species. Mice must be the most common choice, the general consensus being that an average healthy cat needed ten a day, followed – especially in the past – by rats and then perhaps rabbits. But pigeons and partridges (as we have seen with trout) still have their devotees. Come to think about it, Eneri (met in Chapter 5) was once in hiding in an apple orchard I was working in. He watched me approach a tree under which he must have known there was a young family of partridges. As I got too close for the mother bird's comfort, she rapidly led away her brood of nearly a score of chicks, one of which Eneri grasped and immediately ate. Such a large number of chicks close together would have made an easy catch. No doubt several were caught over the next days.

Partly because I could never face rabbit after seeing so many struggle and die deformed with myxomatosis, a cat has never presented me with anything for our table. But I have been given gifts in most unexpected circumstances. Driving through the deep countryside, one frequently sees the occasional cat, sometimes on a fencing post, looking for mice in the grass below. In my lonely days, I used to stop the car to see if such a cat would talk. They seldom do if you open the window right by them, but park a few yards away and stand still and they often become curious, though torn between you and finishing their kill. Twice in the same area of Devon, though I don't think it was the same cat, the animal wagged its tail, undecided whether to complete its kill or come to see me. It did both, rapidly collecting a mouse and dropping it at my feet as a thank you for passing the time of day.

There can be little countryside not sooner or later explored by a cat, and in its lifetime an energetic animal can kill thousands of mice. Going back to the early days when farm labourers received a mere pittance but the landed gentry were prepared to pay big money for hunting, a reward of up to a shilling was offered for a rat, for rats were known to eat young rabbits and pheasants, and especially take the latter's eggs. It says much about the value system in rural life of bygone days that occasionally the cat could earn more in a week than its owner. It only needed a rat a day to equal the average farm labourer's pay when Britain was reaching the zenith of power under Queen Victoria. And for stealing a shilling you could be hanged or transported.

Woodlands have always challenged cats. Though climbing a tree offers a quick temporary shelter, predators are often not in a hurry and can wait for the cat to descend, while in the past gamekeepers weren't too fussy about using their guns. But it is particularly in woods, though only witnessed by the very patient or lucky, that rabbits, cats and foxes have been seen playing together, romping, jumping over each other, enjoying each other's bluffing tactics. Once accepted as playmates, animals seldom hurt each other.

Even today gypsies sometimes stay just outside woods; in the past they were far more frequent visitors, usually with cats who hunted diligently, feeding themselves and bringing birds and rabbits for the pot ... and, in the distant past, even old, semi-rotting meat that no ordinary people would eat but the gypsy constitution somehow coped with. Kittens were likely to be left behind when the gypsies moved on. W. H. Hudson, from whose *A Shepherd's Life* a few of theses historic examples are cited, recalls how the better part of two centuries ago a family of kittens was abandoned on the outskirts of a village. Villagers didn't want them themselves, yet felt they were too old to drown. The solution in that cruder age? Give them to a ferret to eat. Though probably not supposed to be kinder to the kittens, at least it avoided the waste that hungry workers couldn't stand. Hudson is about the only reliable source we have about aspects of cats in country life as long ago as 1830 – as far back as human memory stretched at the time he was writing.

Moorlands, too, are not totally catless, in the past or today. A cat is especially valued for its company and mousing in remote moorland homes. Even the chicks of our beach's oystercatchers, nesting on the stone walls on the high hills a few miles inland from where we live, are not without casualties from felines.

The seaside might seem to be the environment least likely to attract cats, yet I have seen them in Scotland and Devon right down on the rocks at low tide, when bird life abounds and there are ample hiding places for stalking. Once I saw a hare dash at high speed along our sandy Moray Firth beach at low tide as though he were late for a game at the golf course further along. The grey-and-white cat that had obviously been out-chased was – typically for its self-respect – pretending it was only down on the beach to sun itself.

A long-haired tabby cat frequently descended the red sandstone cliffs beside the railway on the famous Sea Wall between Dawlish and Teignmouth. While he might have caught mice or birds on the cliffs, on the wall itself he seemed more interested in entertainment and ingratiating himself with suitable visitors ... taking not the least notice of the circling seagulls, or them of him. This cat seemed to cross the railway tracks with great care, but many are the stories of cats actually sitting on a rail and losing their life through becoming mesmerised by the approach of a train.

Cats are daily at work in all environments in Britain and most of the rest of the world. Most people regret the birds they catch, but many more mice and rats are killed even today, with enormous economic benefit. During the war, there was a milk powder ration for any cat guarding a store of 250 tons of human or animal food. Taking into account the lives they have saved by alerting people to danger, especially fire and robbers (from America come reports of rapists being attacked and sent packing by cats defending their mistresses), there is no doubt that as a species the cat has honoured its part of the 4000-year-old bargain Desmond Morris talks about on page 127. For our part we humans — especially in the Western world — have undoubtedly become softer and therefore much kinder, giving cats a fuller and more comfortable life.

If I am honest, I might have hoped that a cat would move in with us. That would have overcome the need to reach a formal agreement to have one with my new dog-loving wife Sheila. But there was a good reason why it didn't happen. The wood next door was infested with feral cats, fed by a well-meaning neighbour who couldn't bear the thought of them going hungry. Fed they might have been, but they could not stand human proximity let alone company. Whenever we were in the garden, there always seemed to be a couple of poor-looking specimens scampering away. In fairness to our neighbour, she had them humanely trapped so they could be dressed or neutered. Since they led short unloved lives, they gradually faded away. Meantime, my catless state continued.

In the Western world, today's most unfortunate cats are certainly those emaciated ones living rough and tough, seeking out a meagre existence during their short lives. They are usually found in cities and notably Continental ones. Rome and Venice are notorious for their appalling cat colonies. You now have to go to the Far East or to the really backward countries of the developing world to find cats used as human food. But the Continentals: 'For goodness sake, nobody feeds them, it spoilt my holiday,' a tourist who spent time in both Venice and Florence told me. In a cheap Italian hotel, at dinner one evening I watched people at neighbouring tables furtively transferring food from plate to bag to be given to the hungry strays later.

My wife Sheila and I have been guilty of it, most recently in the old capital of Malta, the Silent City of Medina, where – by the bus station just outside the city walls – thin, expectant (and slightly fatter expecting) cats of various colours lined up for our offerings, the bravest first, the timid on inadequate rations of leftover scraps. How could we ensure that our remaining food fed the most needy mouths? It is a problem familiar to those who feed wildlife and especially birds.

Over many visits I have certainly found most Continental cats, even domesticated ones, less inquisitive and friendly than those in the English-speaking Western world. It naturally depends on what part of the Continent. Mediterranean countries have the poorest cats, while at the other extreme Scandinavian cats are not unlike our own. I recall that, while picking wild raspberries beside a lake in

Norway, a tabby walked past and responded to my call. Instantly, its owner, a girl of about nine whom I had not previously noticed, picked it up and held it in her arms, proffering its white undercarriage for a stroke. My wife then appeared with camera: we all co-operated in the sort of encounter that enriches any day.

Switzerland is another good country for casual cat encounters. There was an especially charming meeting in a backstreet in the pretty village of Gandria hanging over the steep cliffs looking out across Lake Lugano. Two abundantly fed cats, a huge tabby moggie – so large I first took it to be a Main Coon – and a handsome grey, instantly responded to my voice by lying on adjoining walls, purring away in their seductive curves. Though twice the grey cat tried to fetch my hand back with its velvety paw, each only rose when I switched attention, one wanting to see exactly what was going on with the other. Such jealous curiosity didn't stop their own enjoyment when my hand returned to the right tummy.

It was just outside Switzerland, in France under the shadow of Strasbourg's cathedral, that I first came across an organ grinder with a cat instead of the traditional monkey. These days the cat – a large pure grey – would attract a more responsive succession of head strokers than would a monkey whose unpredictable behaviour might have made people nervous. And once you have stroked the organ grinder's cat's head, it is hard not to put coins in the receptacle. That cat was tied into a basket on the owner's bicycle while he turned the instrument's handle.

Just inside Switzerland, at the approach to Geneva station, a large fluffy pale stone-coloured cat called Vanille was actually in the basket attached to the organ where years ago a monkey would have been sure to sit. The monkey would have been on a lead, but free to jump out, prance around and – if well trained – catch coins and take them in its mouth to its owner or collecting box.

Vanille, on comfy bedding, hardly took any notice of the line of people who came up to stroke her. When, however, I asked the owner her name and he said it clearly, she immediately stood to attention and peered into his eyes wondering what next.

'Is she tied in?' I asked.

'Oh no. I don't believe in strapping cats in. She's perfectly free to come and go. Matter of fact, if I spend too long talking when I go to coffee and she thinks it's time I came back on duty, she comes to fetch me.' There was obviously a close affinity, which I assumed was one cat to one human until he added: 'I've 24 cats in total; the largest is enormous, 13 kilos. They're all rescue cats. Vanille was just four days old when she came to me. She's now ten years and three months.'

Here was a real cat lover, and playing evocative music, too. 'You know what?' he broke in, steadily turning the organ's handle, 'Cats: if you have one you don't need a psychologist. And if cats ruled the world, there might be occasional scraps but none of the deep-seated problems human governments create.' After that, perhaps because we'd won the confidence of her owner, Vanille began purring for us. What else could have given such joy outside a railway station? (On our return home I discovered that Celia Haddon's *Daily Telegraph* column on pets had previously included a letter complaining about a 'heavily sedated' organ grinder's cat in Geneva;

obviously Vanille. 'Relaxed not sedated,' said Celia. 'With meticulous training from early kittenhood, it is possible to get a cat that is unworried by crowds.')

There were other Swiss cats, too, such as a minute all-black with only a third of a tail, who rapidly accepted an invitation to join me on a wall in the mountain village of Gaatard. Every time I stroked her just in front of her excuse for a tail, she nuzzled into my armpit, chirping and purring. What owner's heart had she won? Switzerland is a safe country, even for cats.

It was while watching the progress of a paddle steamer on one of Switzerland's larger lakes against a majestic mountain backdrop that I wandered into reverie, thinking about love in all its contexts. It was the kind of setting and peaceful yet invigorating moment when things pop into perspective. As it happens I had been reading about a cat so passionately attached to and protective of his owner that it had been banned from innumerable pubs. The enormous ginger tom went everywhere on the owner's shoulder, but jumped down to attack anyone who appeared to be threatening or even just unfriendly to him. Here is an extreme example of Sara's behaviour when she took my side so firmly that even if I pushed my daughter in play she bit her legs. And in a pub, of course, boisterous talk might easily be misunderstood by a cat. However precious, the love of a cat can often become blind or narrowly focused. It does no one, and least of all cats themselves, any good pretending they have a large brain and excel at human virtues. We might be excused occasionally calling them our baby, for they depend on us and are (usually) delightful, but they are not human substitutes and it does no good to treat them as such.

'But how can you say such things?' someone is bound to ask. The answer is that while of course cats are part of God's creation, they don't read the Bible. If they did, their interpretation would surely be extremely fundamental. They don't read anything or even absorb the TV news. At the height of the crisis, Iraq wasn't a word that meant anything to them. Blair, Bush, Howard are not evocative names for them (lucky things, we might say). They lack our power of thought and discretion ... a force we humans admittedly frequently misuse.

Cats can help us develop wider love; most short stories featuring them seem to involve them fostering love between humans. They are part of God's creation and can help us fulfil ourselves in whatever way with whatever beliefs we might have individually. Beyond that cats are a hobby. Hobbies are important, but they need to be seen for what they are.

Playing golf or cuddling a cat might be complementary or alternatives along with pastimes such as stamp collecting, gardening and operating a model railway. In this sense the fact that a cat is a live animal really makes no difference, the only rider being that even if you are a cat hater you should respect the wellbeing of living things and avoid giving pain. But then golf clubs and stamp albums don't greet you warmly when you come in – or help turn a house into a home.

All of which might seem trite moralising, but it actually goes deeper than might be immediately realised. Cats may be warm-hearted living things, but treat them as human substitutes and you're in difficulties. Which reminds me that once I was invited into the home of a neighbour well known for his philandering. Mitzie, his fluffy white cat, was also a flirt, adept at making a fool of me as I moved across the lawn while she progressively laid herself down in a rolling curve just out of reach.

'You like cats?' asked my neighbour when Mitzie came into the room tail up and I reached to stroke her. In all seriousness, he added: 'I prefer women.'

As I say, treat cats as human substitutes and you're in trouble. Accept that and you are released from inhibition to make the most of them – as cats.

As I remained without a cat of my own, occasional encounters in the streets and other people's homes were important and I consoled myself with much reading. While cat owners are almost as varied as their charges, it became clear that in the Western world, authors and musicians were among the very first to appreciate what cats offer, their pets enjoying what until the 1930s or even 1950s would have been a rare level of comfort if not luxury. Incidentally, those who might have doubted the accuracy of my remarks about how it is only in recent times that men have been able to admit to being cat lovers might be interested to know – it was extra confirmation for me since I read it after writing my remarks – that W. H. Hudson spoke of how unusual it was for men to show their feelings for a cat. Cats were things you just had, ideally to work at keeping down mice and rabbits – and often donating food to a hungry family.

Though one writer said, 'Cats are dangerous companions for writers because cat watching is a near-perfect method of writing avoidance,' it is easy to explain why authors are attracted by saying that writing is a solo, lonely business and that a cat makes for good company. But it is slightly subtler than that. A compulsion to write endlessly doesn't produce the best results; one needs to respect one's own humanity and needs. Thus, far from being a time-wasting distraction, a great view is good value. Even glancing at it for a few seconds helps perspective and clarity.

An interruption by a cat is usually similarly helpful. It lightens the mood without breaking continuity. It is much less disturbing than human interruption because humans tell you their own thoughts, remind you of something that needs to be born in mind, or – worst of all – ask you just what you're writing, which usually produces an abbreviated reply sounding silly and results in loss of confidence. Cats may sit on the manuscript you are correcting, which may be a bit of a nuisance, but they don't interrupt your thoughts far less demand to know exactly what you're doing. They never argue about subject matter or syntax. It is because they don't know, can't understand, yet are fascinated usually in a respectful kind of way, that they are such good company. In any event, many top authors have been cat lovers and quite a few (Edgar Allan Poe's dark tale of 'The Black Cat' is the first to come to mind) have immortalised their pets.

Few publishers are themselves authors, so explaining the link with cats here is more difficult, but the numbers involved are anyway much smaller, so chance plays a stronger role. Perhaps it is only a particular kind of publisher who is a cat enthusiast? Maybe it is just tradition – or again, chance? If it is tradition, without doubt it was established by Michael Joseph, a brilliant, world-famous publisher who, though not generally much of a writer himself, produced a bestselling *Charles: The Story of a Friendship*. A Siamese, Charles, or to give him his full name

Charles O'Malley, was added to Michael Joseph's 'collection' of cats as long ago as 1930, when few people even knew of the breed. The 1931 edition of the *Encyclopaedia Britannica* at least recognised its existence, though somewhat curiously: 'By far the most remarkable of the Old World domesticated breed is the royal Siamese cat ... extremely delicate.'

Michael had become enchanted with their talkativeness and sharp interest in everything going on around them after getting to know one belonging to a friend. He describes the journey back from the breeder with his six-week-old kitten one sunny August day:

> *Such a funny, enchanting little thing he was! His peaky head and paws looked just as if they had been slightly singed in front of a fire. His bright blue eyes, unaccustomed to the sharply changing light which flashed through the windows of the moving train, blinked incessantly; and he raised his voice – a blend of croak and squeak, and very audible – in one continuous protest against the strange things which were happening to him. He was not in the least afraid. Already I was accepted as a friend and protector. Between his out-bursts he rubbed his head against my hand and purred bravely. But I was glad when the journey ended, as I always am when I have a cat with me, for it is easy to share their apprehension and discomfort at such times.*

Charles led a complicated life, including army service, and got involved in everything going on in successive homes. From the book, we catch a whiff of what armed conflict does for our cats. In World War I, for instance, when Michael Joseph was serving in the trenches, Scissors, 'a bonny little black and white cat', simply arrived one day and remained until Michael was moved to another part of the line. He was last seen trotting across no-man's-land: 'I can only hope that the Bavarians across the way treated him kindly.' Evacuated from London in World War II, Charles suffered the indignity of a strong-willed pregnant Siamese queen moving in and taking over everything he favoured. Of his ultimate demise, in the dark days of 1942, we are told:

> *In the midst of a devastating war with all its wide-spread human suffering the death of a cat may seem an unimportant matter. Those who are indifferent to animals or merely tolerate them will doubtless think so, but anyone who has intimately known and loved an animal and has been honoured with that animal's friendship and devotion will, I believe, agree with me that it is not easy to bear the loss.*

It was partly through reading what joy cats had brought to other authors and publishers that I decided the time really had come to get another of my own. Another reason was that it seemed silly to spend the rest of my life honouring Sara without enjoying how another cat would differ from her. Yet perhaps the real reason was that Sheila persuaded me I needed a cat. I recalled from our friendship over 40 years earlier that Sheila was a dog rather than a cat person – though many years ago her first husband had become incredibly close to Jimmy, the stray who came to settle, introduced on page 33.

Life for me had changed dramatically. I had sold David & Charles and moved to Scotland. While living alone, I would certainly have welcomed a cat, but was frequently away from home. Some evenings I had dinner at our local hotel on the international wining and dining circuit, where the grandeur but not the friendliness was echoed by Auberon, the Persian with an inferiority complex who I discovered ganged up with the over-fed King Charles to bully the gentler white fluffy Zambenflöte. When Zambenflöte saw me arriving, it surreptitiously followed me into the dining room and hid under the table offering what it has to be admitted was cupboard love for titbits. Poor cat: it had so loved an earlier dachshund. Like most self-respecting cats, Zambenflöte hated being left out. It stole the show, or rather brought it to a stop, when it walked into that large dining room during one of its periodic changes into the theatre of our local Performing Arts Guild.

Following remarriage, I expected that after I had disposed of a successful magazine business employing up to sixteen people in our busy house, another move would be necessary. But Sheila and her William, a grand old Westie, took root as though they had always lived on the shores of the Moray Firth. William paraded proprietarily along the bank overlooking promenade, beach and sea, occasionally breaking into a trot to catch up on what was happening below. William was an enjoyable dog. 'But you're always stopping to talk to cats and talking about them,' said Sheila. 'You need one.' And I naturally realised, that helpful to a point as casual encounters with other people's cats had been, it was distinctly not the same as having one's own cat. So now ... expectant excitement.

Another cat to be; another chance to decide what kind; another delicious period of dreaming of owning and being owned by short-hairs, long-hairs, moggies, exotics and all manner of rarities.

Cat magazines became compelling reading, titillating the emotions, supposing this and that. If all the cats we had more or less decided upon were put together, we would have made one of those newspaper stories about vast feline menageries. Yet we were only interested in a single cat with whom we could bond closely.

One day it was going to be a Somali, which *Your Cat* said was a sweet-talking guy who would charm our socks off. 'If the foxiness of the Somali doesn't bowl you over, his soft voice and zest for life will.' Next day perhaps a British Shorthair: 'Cuddle factor is paramount ... gentle lap cats who enjoy affection.' Day three it might be a Bengal: 'Exotic looks coupled with good manners but with a streak of mischief ... a unique individual.' Day four a less emotional but usually very satisfying moggie, definitely grey. Then a Birman with princely paws and noble nature: 'Take him into your palace and he'll soon be lord of the sofa ... Loves human company and is very intelligent. With very little effort he will soon have you eating out of his regal paws.'

So it went on, sometimes with breeds we hadn't previously realised existed. A few ultra-glamorous cats, such as the Chinchilla, and those with unusual features such as the bare-looking Devon Rex with tight curls, and the tail-less Manx, we easily passed over, no doubt little realising what joy we were rejecting. I have never favoured flat-faced Persians, and it is often said that moggie tortoiseshells have less than average tolerance for life, because of their skin or its colouring. But again what fun we may have missed. Eventually the choice narrowed to a Siamese-type. No other pure Siamese could touch Sara.

Tonkinese almost won the day for us. It perhaps is the breed I now most regret not having. Burmese, the sparkling champagne of cats, also came into the consideration. They are lovely and intelligent, but perhaps a shade too demanding and naughty?

Eventually the choice fell on Balinese: 'Bright, intelligent, inquisitive, independent and playful.' An article quoting various people's happy experiences with them decided it. A Balinese with fluffy tail would be harmoniously vocal but, slightly dog-like, follow us and need our company rather than setting a challenging agenda. Or so our naïve thoughts ran.

Chapter 9

SKYE AND ARRAN

We nearly had to decide all over again what kind of cat we would like, for no breeder seemed to have Balinese kittens for months to come. Then fate played its part. Our last hope was a breeder at Wootton Bassett near Swindon. We had planned a semi-work trip to Bath, and thought it would be best to give a kitten a long settling-in period immediately on our return, before our next trip four months later. The breeder, Elaine Robinson, said she had only one pure Balinese, who wouldn't be ready for a new home until the very day after we had already fixed to travel back to Scotland.

'Well, I'm sure one day won't matter,' she conceded. The remaining kitten was a boy.

We agreed to drive over from Bath once we were there, and – if we liked what we saw – arrange that he who was to be named Arran would a few days later be handed over to us at Swindon station for an evening train to London and sleeper up to the Highlands.

Then we had doubts. Were Balinese so human-orientated that one on its own might be seriously unhappy? Especially as we were away for long periods? 'You really wanted a girl, so why don't we also have the other one in the litter even though she's not pure Balinese?' asked Sheila. Sweet words. Elaine had described her as 'Variant: Balinese in temperament but with short Siamese hair instead of the boy's true Balinese long fur and great fluffy tail.'

It did not take much to have me on the phone again. Elaine was delighted to sell them both and said they would always be good friends. But at one point I could hardly hear her. 'What's that noise?' I asked.

'Oh, that's Arran speaking his mind. You wouldn't want two like him. He's very vocal. The girl's much quieter, though good fun.' What were we letting ourselves in for?

Arran greeted us noisily when we made the journey from Bath to Wootton Bassett, but Skye, infinitely smaller, immediately gained my love with her deep-blue eyes so large that they almost seemed slightly to protrude from her minute white face. She looked at me intently, pleadingly connecting we two creatures of such different size, age and species that we might become as one. Meanwhile the siblings' dad was slaughtering a paper mouse, their mum engaged in domestic duties.

Our visit coincided with Swindon's cat show at which – although progress through the aisles was delayed by other cats, notably Orientals, clamouring for attention – we naturally concluded we had made the perfect choice. A single cage would do for the journey home and was delivered to Elaine, with whom we fixed the exact time for the handover on Swindon station. Meanwhile the final touches had been added to what would become the outside part of their home in Nairn. Especially because of business vehicles dashing up and down the drive, we decided to make them basically indoor cats, but with a cat flap leading to a sizable run including a raised viewing platform reached by a long tree branch.

We travelled to Swindon by High Speed Train and waited ... until a wail emerged from the steps leading up to the platform. Every time we spoke to Arran, he noisily had the last word. What would other passengers think?

That was the question that dominated the journey, the first part on another HST. It wasn't that we minded what people thought, but were fascinated by the sharply different reactions to these two mini-beasts with maxi-voices – Skye wasn't as naturally talkative but could more than hold her own – placed on a table just inside the end gangway door of a busy first-class coach. As people passed, joining and alighting, visiting the loo or buying refreshments, it was fascinating forecasting what the reaction would be. Predictably, proportionately more women than men, and all children, smiled or talked to the cats and commented, 'You've got bundles of fun there,' or 'They're going to change your lives'. Again, predictably, some of those who pretended not to notice were the hard-looking businesswomen striving to be more masculine than men in a man's world. One or two of them then delightfully melted – as did roughly one in three men whether dressed in pinstripes or tweed. Arran lapped up all attention, answering everyone. Skye looked ... and looked. Not an everyday happening in the business section of an HST.

Into a taxi and, on a summer evening, then a break on the grass outside Euston station while we ate a sandwich supper, Arran still chattering, Skye looking and taking it all in. Neither was much interested in food, though they did drink. Neither seemed particularly lost. It was as though they knew they had to travel from one end of Britain to the other but were not quite sure what it would be like.

On an earlier occasion we had pre-booked Sheila's Westie dog to travel on the sleeper, paying a £40 'heavy cleaning' supplement, which that night's conductor said wasn't really necessary. Tonight's different conductor – we had booked the sleeper before knowing we were bringing kittens back – expostulated: 'Animals. You'll have to pay £40 for heavy cleaning.' Paying for earplugs for neighbouring passengers might have been fairer. By now our new charges were sleepy. Lights out and Arran was silenced. Not so Skye. She wasn't going to miss seeing anything and screamed till the light was on again. Hardly going to sleep at all, she stared all night, not distressed but needing to stay in touch. After breakfast was brought to the cabin, we took them out of their cage. When stroked, Skye purred and stared into our eyes. Arran chatted, wriggled and clean disappeared; there were harrowing moments wondering if he could slip into a void forever before we rescued him from a deep recess under the bed.

They took well to train travel, but both howled in the taxi from Inverness to Nairn. Holding their paws gave reassurance but not silence as they echoed each other's plaintive wailings. How could we be so cruel? The real cruelty was to Dave the taxi who could hardly make himself heard as, in his usual way, he tried to tell us about unusual fares he had recently had in the car.

Taken out of their cages at home, Skye and Arran immediately knew that this was where they now belonged, saw where their toilets were placed, where they would be fed, and the tiny bed by the Aga into which they soon climbed, entangling each other with their paws for comfort, the pair of them only occupying a fraction of the space. Arran slept soundly; Skye fitfully, her eyes always open when someone — or William the Westie — passed. William was accepted as part of their new home. They soon cuddled up to him in his bed; he always accepted anything that came his way.

Later that day Skye had her first purr lying on my left arm. She had to be on top of it, not tucked into my jacket as Sara had been when new. She couldn't bear not to see what was going on. From the start she let me hold her front paw in a way that Sara never did, and seemed to like our holding her tail. But extinguish her vision and there was immediate protest. Arran didn't seem to mind — or for that matter much notice — what we did to him, but quickly cottoned on to our talking to him and never failed to answer back. How could brother and sister be so different in just about every way? Bigger differences were to emerge.

A few days later we invited some cat-loving friends to a welcome party. Arran couldn't conceive how anyone wouldn't want to give him a personal welcome and cuddle. Skye kept close to me, studying the visitors and Arran's social round, but disinclined to follow.

Then it was a trip to the vet. Noisily announcing our arrival, Arran was put out that other waiting customers didn't abandon their dogs, rabbits and hamsters to talk to him. Skye kept her eyes on me. 'You've a lively one there,' said the vet about Arran. 'But is that one all right? She's the smallest I've ever seen. Hope she's going to be okay.' His stethoscope proved that she had nothing vital missing. 'But I'd like to keep an eye on her. She's obviously the runt of the litter.' A few months later he admitted how wrong he had been, for Skye — always the greedier eater — was already the sturdier of the pair. When they were neutered, though hers was the greater operation, she seemed the least upset.

'That's a woman for you,' became a common comment. Yes, the female of the species is generally more matter-of-fact and practical. Men and women should undoubtedly be given equal opportunity, but it is ridiculous to pretend that sex makes no difference. Just as when, still in my arms, my daughter began showing more interest in clothes and fashion than her brother will ever do, so Skye was immediately fascinated by our appearance. She always shows intense interest, watching if the right outfit will be chosen, when Sheila is getting dressed for dinner out. Arran, bless him, wouldn't notice if Sheila went in her underclothes, any more than I notice the latest styles adopted by the staff. I once asked my hairdresser where the person I'd made the appointment with that morning was. 'It's me,' she declared. She'd changed her hairstyle.

In a hundred and one ways Arran and Skye have behaved just as you would expect a boy and girl to do. It is uncanny.

A slow developer, Arran certainly wouldn't have passed his school certificate. He has always taken greater risks and wouldn't have passed his driving test first time either. He more frequently falls, gets shut in — and panics. He is less practical, yet if he really wants something he persists until he succeeds. He has developed the more adventurous games, showing extraordinary creativity in the way he convinces himself a screwed-up piece of paper actually is a mouse and that he's left it alone sufficiently long for it to forget him, so that he can surprise it afresh. And one by one, he has learnt virtually all the tricks that were unique to Skye. If he didn't take quite so many risks, with his creativity and determination – noting what goes down well in others and popular with everyone – he'd almost be managing director material though, come to think of it, he'd be too trusting and probably a victim of fraud.

Skye, on the other hand, would make a sound, level-headed line manager, always aware of exactly what is happening around her and prepared to search the house to find us, or Arran should he have gone missing. She would also command loyalty from a tighter group of people, but has no wish to conquer the world. She is just as keen (maybe keener) on climbing to the top shelf, more sure-footed and less likely to knock things over. She is a precision machine and in the wild would undoubtedly be the more skilful hunter. When she finds herself in a tight position, we love watching her carefully come out backwards, putting her right back paw out to feel for support below.

In their different ways, they both love being the centre of attention, but Skye is more anxious (and content) to command that of just a few of us, notably myself whose sweet nothings are especially dear to her. As part of her bonding with us, she has always needed to give us presents. If I am still busy on the typewriter after she has tired of dabbing the keys, she quietly disappears to reappear a few minutes later with a cacophony to wake the dead. She has sought out one of the coloured toy ferrets pooled around the house. The blood-curdling noises stop as she drops it at my feet, sometimes on our bed or outside the closed door for me to find later. It is less disturbing than receiving live, maimed or dead rabbits, voles and birds. Yet she frequently finds flies, daddy-long-legs and bees and wasps to chase. Even if her attention is focused elsewhere, the smallest insect passing or making the slightest sound sets her chasing. A dozen or so mice and voles a year are stupid enough to be caught in their run enclosed by fine meshing.

While earlier mice and voles were caught by Skye, now the conquests seem equally shared. We can tell when it is Arran, for part of his killing ritual has always been to help feed himself. His mouse is added to the bowl to give variety to the dry food. More recently he has cottoned on to the multi-coloured ferrets, and now occasionally adds one of them to the food bowl, no doubt thinking he is saving our purse. As for screwed-up paper 'mice', once he has tired of retrieving and batting, they go into the water bowl. He gazes at them steadily unfurling. When they cease to move, they are 'dead'.

Sometimes the pair work together like a couple of well-acquainted criminals. Arran loves opening doors — a pursuit of great joy in its own right. If a bin or other obstacle is placed in front of a door to prevent it being opened, he tries moving it if only a fraction of a centimetre at a time. He uses different well-tried techniques for different doors. He will push or crash himself against one repeatedly to see if it will unlatch. He jumps up at handles and latches; again, time is no obstacle. If only he can get a door fractionally ajar, he will work with his hooked paw endlessly to lever it open, however gradually. Skye watches encouragingly, but taking no active part.

As soon as a door is open, however, Arran moves onto his next challenge while Skye climbs into the cupboard to see what can be found – and eaten. Many a morning we have discovered the food placed in their dishes untouched, but several pouches and bags in the cupboard where their food is kept carefully nibbled through if we've inadvertently left it unbolted. It no doubt tastes better than the identical food offered in their dishes. Yet, though Arran's patience is endless, he is also a realist and if finally defeated simply moves to another challenge.

Arran's increasing repertoire of tricks has been to understand the difference between the front door and our internal ringing codes on the bell of the same ex-railway signalling apparatus. Back door bells mean nothing to him, since business people arriving that way seldom come into the house. The front door denotes visitors: curious strangers worth investigating for they might cuddle him. Two rings when I am in my study means that our own meal is ready – a signal for me and of no relevance to Arran. The next identical two-bell signal is interpreted as his message to come down to the kitchen. He never fails to arrive, and quickly too. When he first comes in, naturally there is a greeting, and a two-way conversation is kept up until we have had enough and leave the last word to him.

Not that Skye is silent. She is actually readier to use her voice to request something – like 'Open the door', 'Pick me up', 'Dinnertime', 'I want some treats' – and to make long love speeches. So we don't go head over first falling over her, she also meows to warn that she is going to collapse on the stairs for a luxuriating multi-level tickle. But she doesn't engage in long talks for their own sake.

Communication from her always has a meaning. If it is a soft half-meow when I approach her should she be lying somewhere comfortably, it means 'Hullo, and yes you can stroke or tickle me'. In such cases, she's usually purring before she speaks.

In my study, they both crave undivided attention and a hair-raising ride on my swivel chair. Skye usually comes first but used to slink away if Arran even threatened to beat her to it. Jealousy is in-built, yet with a firm hand and sweetly mouthing both of their names, they have finally began enjoying the occasional ride side by side, both purring.

Though they are brother and sister, their extreme difference is emphasised by Skye always being a cat while Arran can't decide if he's dog or cat. When he's not moving in a poncy semi-circle, or (when trying to do something not allowed) slowly flattening himself as though hiding from a mouse and so is, presumably, also invisible to us, he walks like a dog and is all too ready to come to heel. He retrieves, and frequently stretches himself up on his hind paws to take a good look. Why bother to jump when you can hold your head 2 to 3 feet up? But his speciality is jumping onto one of our shoulders. The mere prospect starts him purring – our warning that he is coming airborne. He flies up to 8 feet in a perfectly calculated arc.

Skye prefers to be picked up. I've never known a cat so enjoy being handled. Often when picked up she climbs from arm to shoulder then round my neck and stays up there as I eat, sit at my desk or move around the house (I call her my scarf). If she wriggles in mid journey it is because she is contemplating the one jump she is in danger of making – to somewhere higher up, too far up for her otherwise to reach. Then I steady her by holding her tail which, as already said, she likes, whereas if you even touch Arran's tail he looks at your hand and the tail concluding it is a mistake but not quite sure if its the hand's or tail's fault.

As well as being healthier and living longer, cats today are probably bonding in more discerning ways with their owners. This sharpens the focus on the fact that they have only a limited range of ways in which to demonstrate their affection. Possibly longer and more sophisticated life will eventually result in further evolution, making future cats brainier than they are today. Meanwhile that part of the brain devoted to social communication, and not motivated by hunting, is limited, which results in odd semi-sexual behaviour. Celia Haddon says that her popular 'Petsubjects' column in Saturday's *Daily Telegraph* sometimes reads like *The News of the World*. She writes about a male cat who, when worked up about something, frequently mounts a female simply as a means of communicating emotion. Arran frequently holds down Skye by the nape of her neck, which naturally she doesn't like. But then she might like it even less if I responded when she exposes her backside, tail out of the way, and makes a treading movement. Technically it is known as lordosis, the position inviting mating. It is her way of conveying trust and, of course, non-sexual emotion.

If evolution does indeed ultimately increase the size of the cat's social brain, the first sign will no doubt be an extended range of body language. Meanwhile we need to learn how frustrating present limitations are for intelligent cats, and make allowances. Dogs are a lot worse at sniffing human's sexual parts, but I have to accept that when Skye brushes against my crotch she is just making the most of the limited range of ways of communication open to her.

The range actually seems quite large: different meows, a lot of tail language, opening and closing of eyes, and concentrated listening or shutting off. (Cat language is discussed more fully in the following chapter.) Skye runs after me when excited, stretches slowly when waking up, the fur on her back ripples when she's hoping to be picked up. We should feel privileged that cats work so hard to convey their feelings, but there is one thing they find difficult to show: how much they love us. Since it is so recently in anthropological history that they were all just wild animals with only survival instincts, they suffer in the same way as uptight husbands who lack the emotional ability to speak the words that tell their wife they love her.

In the same way that older people have seen dogs steadily show better road sense, in our own lifetime we have noticed how much more cats do socialise with humans in different ways. For example, though it would be hard to prove, almost certainly the average middle-aged domestic cat understands more words than their great-grandparents. Historical comparisons are hindered by the paucity of serious cat literature until our own time, but even in fiction we see modern cats display more emotion and understanding than those in the classic novels of Victorian and earlier days. As was said earlier, humans could often help improve communication by using simple techniques and language, for example sticking to a single word to convey a meaning such as 'Soon'. The most universally understood word is perhaps 'Sorry'. Just like Sara, Skye and Arran almost welcome a minor injury to hear me say it and concentrate on comforting them at least for a moment.

To this Sheila would add that if evolution is going to make cats more intelligent, there has to be negative as well as positive learning. Arran is one of those cats far easier to make understand new things than to stop silly — or is it just irritating in our eyes? — behaviour. Typically cat-like, he waits patiently outside a door. He purposefully trots in when the drawing room door is opened for our evening round the fire together. If one or other of us opens the door to come in a second later, Arran wants out. Skye has learnt the meaning of 'Fire' — a drawing-room source of warmth — albeit her learning needs freshening up after each summer break when we are without fires even in the north of Scotland. 'Fire' has her trotting rapidly downstairs to take her position on the rug in front of the grate. She has sussed that if the guard is in front of the flames, she is safe from mildly explosive logs and their sparks. If we settle down she will happily snuggle in front of the fire for an hour or two, only rising when it becomes time for her nightly purrs in my arms. Yet if the door is opened, or left the tiniest bit ajar, she also might dart off as though happiness is only available on the other side. It might be an hour or more before she returns, when — carrying a gift of one of their 'ferrets' — she loudly complains about being shut out. Sometimes her enthusiasm to reconnect and have another session in my arms makes her absence worthwhile.

As yet, it is only in self-survival ways (including hunting and food), not the search for heavenly contentment, that cats seem to think ahead. But that is not fully correct either, for — no doubt based on the patience instinctive in hunting

– cats will exploit all kinds of dodges to get their own way. Celia Haddon tells how tabby Rufus uses his hypnotic stare to make mere humans feel so uncomfortable on his favourite rocking chair that they find themselves giving it up, even unconsciously moving to the floor. Chester has a different ploy when turned off his favourite chair. He demands to be let out in a hurry and, as soon as the chair is vacated, dashes back to it.

In one way or another, nearly all cat owners are trained by their pets. Recent examples in the 'Petsubjects' column include Edward, a ginger tom, living in sheltered accommodation, who makes sure breakfast is served promptly by swinging on the bedroom alarm cord; and Polly, a fluffy ginger, who determines which days she will have tinned or dry food by meowing at the appropriate separate cupboards in which they are stored.

Skye constantly delays me starting work or going out by lying in a circle on my desk or by my feet at the front door. Arran collapses on the first tread of the stairs, and paws the empty dry food bowl by my desk. How true: dogs have owners, cats have staff. But then dogs merely think they are human, cats that they are God.

Are these all demonstrations of mere self-preservation? Perhaps not, unless self-preservation (of the ego, that is) depends on being the centre of attention. When it comes to food, along with many cats, Arran does show the gift of foresight: he knows that once we have gone to bed, no more food will be provided that night. He becomes agitated as we make our final preparations for going upstairs. It is not that he is actually hungry. As soon as he sees the food put out, and has sniffed it, he dashes through the puss-flap to their run. But he must see and sniff the food to believe it. Just self-preservation?

If their intelligence really does increase with their basic character remaining the same, consider what being a cat owner will entail in future. What elaborate games of chess, what infinite varieties of checkmate, might be played out. 'Thank you, they're already far too clever,' said one cat lover to whom I put this thesis. So they are, in their own (restricted) ways. We hear of cats waking people up, saying when and what they'll eat, whether their owners can sit in their favourite chairs, work without interruptions, talk on the phone for more than two minutes before all hell breaks loose, have to sprint out of the house to prevent being followed, not to mention display ornaments in safe (in human terms) places, keep the toilet door locked to stop it being opened and the loo roll torn to shreds, and have to abandon wallpaper in favour of emulsioned walls. We cannot throw unwanted boxes away because of the pleasure they give or open our Christmas presents without the cats presiding ... actually we aren't so much staff as slaves.

However, as cats get cleverer it will not be a one-way process. While no doubt humans will basically remain their slaves, more useful tasks might well come to be performed by cats. 'Switch the oven on at twelve o'clock, please.' If that sounds far fetched, Ann Bruce of Louth in Lincolnshire claims that Oliver, a ginger tom who came with her partner, is an effective alarm clock. 'Tell him the time you need to be woken.' Which, when put to the test he duly did, persistently pawing her face and meowing at the stated time next morning.

I have heard of cats waking up children if they don't start getting ready for school at the same time as the others, and there have been regular reports of cats saving human lives when a house has caught fire. Then there was Jenny, who repeatedly roused her owner in an atypically persistent way in between running to and from the daughter's closed bedroom door. Eventually the owner was compelled to open it, and found the youngster gasping for breath with pneumonia. Though it was touch and go for a time, another life had been saved. It is also said that cats might do more to entertain us. One report says that acrobatic Bengals may soon attract larger crowds to a cat show. Who can tell in what other useful ways they will serve us?

Punishing a cat to make it change its ways is likely to remain outside the realms of possibility. Training will always mean patiently encouraging them to make it worth their while to do what is required. Maybe if their brains develop and their capacity for going along with us increases, so will their power to displease?

When it comes to the naughty things cats do, mercifully individuals only make their presence felt in selected unwelcome ways. They don't need to do more, do they?

Install a kitten and within a few weeks honestly ask yourself who is in charge. The only doubt in the case of Skye and Arran was which of them would be top cat, enjoying their station well above that of their owners. Our special delight is that they box and cox for prime position.

Sometimes Skye seems in supreme command, assuming she will have our first attention and that we'll brush Arran aside. That happens especially if the kitchen door is closed to prevent them reaching the rest of the house when we return from a trip away. Untangling their paws, they struggle out of bed and flop decisively in a curve on the kitchen rug. Though Arran is considerably longer, Skye achieves a more seductive curve and general attitude, which implies it will be an honour for us to give her our undivided attention. At other times, Arran, the action man, commands all our notice and none more so than Skye's as she follows his antics – usually with condescending respect, occasionally with sheer admiration. Soon he will be on the wrong side of a door. Maybe they don't have doors in cat heaven. But then it wouldn't be heaven for cats unless there were props for their awkwardness.

Here is a thought: each year cats probably make more lasting converts than do our political parties. It is hard not to resist the temptation of saying that (right side of the door or not) they also give us less hassle. Mark Twain might well have had the way we humans govern ourselves in mind when he said: 'If a man could be crossed with the cat, it would improve man but deteriorate the cat.' But just suppose that cats ultimately became so clever that they started lobbying politicians and then maybe took up politics themselves? A silly idea — but then writers have always fantasised about the strange qualities and powers of felines. And if Mark Twain might seem extreme, think how any man would react if yanked out of bed without warning in the middle of a deep sleep, compared to the cat's usual patience, returning to bed without a word or gesture. 'What, those cats still asleep?' Why shouldn't they be?

Skye and Arran, freshly arrived in my study for a ride on my chair and a helping of the prestigious dry food, bring me back to earth. Now middle-aged in cat terms, they are very different from when we first knew them. Then minute and almost pure white, they are now large and gorgeously coloured. Arran is a true chocolate-point, his dark bits, especially ears and feet, growing steadily darker, while Skye has an increasingly pink face and a smooth light apricot back leading to a thin striped tail. The tail is still little thicker than a thick piece of wire – unless she is frightened or angry, when it bristles out to a broad, colourful brush. Her tummy, which she insists we enjoy tickling, is still pure white. The visual pièce de résistance of the pair is undoubtedly Arran's dark chocolate fluffy tail. Almost everyone comments on it, yet (except when licking it) he scarcely acknowledges it has any connection with him.

Sheila sometimes pretends she still doesn't like cats, but naturally she watches them, talks to them and daily is fascinated by their curious ways. So far I have concentrated on the extraordinary differences between brother and sister. But what might they think about the differences between us? Let us trace the four of us through a typical day.

Sheila is usually first downstairs and finds them waiting on top of the fridge close to the kitchen door. They flop onto the rug, Skye expecting her tummy to be rubbed first. In her ecstasy, she's liable to lever herself out of Sheila's reach. Guess who has to reposition herself? On the other hand, if Arran finds himself out of reach of Sheila's hands, he does his poncy walk around her to resettle closer but on the opposite side. Skye then goes into Sheila's arms or sits on her lap, purring loudly.

They then go back to sleep, and often ignore me when I come into the room. At this early hour of the day, they are Sheila's cats. Indeed, though they do say hello, they are not at all pleased when, occasionally, I am first down. They go back to sleep more soundly in summer, when they spend more of the night outdoors than in winter. Then occasionally they love us both through breakfast.

After breakfast I shout 'Cats' and go upstairs. They feign indifference, but usually have overtaken me by the time I reach the top of the stairs, Arran always being first to race up. If they don't beat me on the stairs, Skye is sure to turn up in my study within a couple of minutes and jump onto my desk chair for a swirl. About one morning a week Arran is very late reporting for work in the study, but the later he is the more enthusiastic his greeting when he does arrive.

As mentioned earlier, these days they sometimes enjoy, indeed now even initiate, a ride together. Then they need their prestigious dry food, eaten eagerly, though they will have left the identical product downstairs. If Sheila comes into my study while I am giving them attention, they are not at all pleased to see her. Her innings is over; they are now my cats who somewhat rudely make their preference known.

They sleep tightly together much of the morning, sometimes in front of a gas fire, other times in their cradle hung from a radiator; it depends on the day's source of heat. In high summer, they bask in sunshine, steadily edging along to remain in its warming rays. Two or three times a morning, however, Skye needs to communicate with me; on cue as I write this, she is at my side, velvet paw on typewriter keys, purring, looking up at me and occasionally talking. If I go through the bedroom to the bathroom, she'll often follow, never wanting to be more than feet away, her head raised enquiringly, her blue eyes wide open. She often jumps onto the bathroom stool, whose much damaged cork top still bears the signs of Sara's front claws – but I've failed in my efforts to encourage Skye to continue the destructive work of her predecessor.

Skye loves being talked to. It doesn't matter what I say, but it must be seriously expressed and sound as though it involves her. Then she'll go to where I keep the treats and 'make her request'. If I ignore her, she must think me incredibly stupid. Next she asks if she can come into my arms, where she'd stay all day if I didn't have work to do. Right now she's alongside the typewriter again wondering what animate thing might make the carriage move at the line's end.

Sheila gives two bells on the railway signalling system, which I acknowledge and go down to lunch. The cats are now entwined in each other's arms in their cradle and ignore the bell and me. But as soon as I get to the kitchen, I ring another two bells and Arran quickly follows. This is his treasured solo time. He nudges me with his head and, his tail held high, talks incessantly, always having the last word, and if asked if he is hungry and would like some 'Fish', becomes delirious. It is much more because we are giving him attention than that he is hungry, for, after a cursory sniff, he ignores the food bowl and comes back to us. He's particularly sad to see us go after we have cleared up, and often tries jumping on one of us to delay us. The fish will be eaten, often pulled out of his dish onto the lino, when we're not looking – or, at least, pretend we're not.

Upstairs, Skye knows she must now come down too. She has to, for any chance of forty winks is ruined by her insisting she should wake me up. I call her, but she ignores me, tucking her head into herself more tightly, pretending sleep though watching me through a slit in her eyes. If I speak to her nicely, she will fully open her eyes and answer, and then wriggle in expectation of being picked up. Once in a while instead she will dash to a chair for a ride, or to the place where I keep her treats. She too would like this to go on all day.

I give Sheila two bells to say that Skye has been put at the top of the stairs. However, if I have forgotten something and have to go down again, Skye collapses between two stairs, and demands to be picked up, which means she'll climb onto my shoulders (I have to wear the same worn, old, tightly woven jacket to prevent damage to a better one) and purr till we reach the kitchen, where she will see what Arran is doing and most likely disturb him or join in. At this point occasionally either or both can be so desperate for company that they snooze with Sheila in her study, though three afternoons a week they share the kitchen with our housekeeper who comes with the scent of her tiny tabby Pepsie, whose own recent loss of appetite was explained when by chance she was seen tucking into a meal outside the kitchen of a hotel. (Pepsie, an inveterate hunter, no doubt told the staff she was starving; she had earlier trespassed on the hospitality of a neighbour.)

An hour later, I call 'Cats' again, and the pair bound upstairs, to repeat the morning's processes. Early evening, when arrangements are more flexible and we might be sitting by the fire or going out, they ignore pleas to come downstairs ... until perhaps I shout 'Fire' to attract them to the drawing room. Yes, again I sometimes have to carry Skye. Eventually they both neatly trot into the drawing room but, as already mentioned, when we start taking in our light supper Arran wants out and back in, often ending up closed out and crying piteously, though very quietly ...

a huge contrast with the super-charged greeting he will give when we eventually get up to let him in.

Though frequently partners in crime, they never jump onto the table where supper is laid out, or indeed onto the dining room or kitchen table if we are eating at it, and expect no titbits. What they do want — nay, need — is cuddles. Skye sits on the arm of my chair until I have finished eating. She's therefore first in position, purring hugely, looking up into my eyes as though all creation were there. Partly because it has to be on my left arm, on which I had an operation, I cannot hold her indefinitely, so she has become used to a series of shorter cuddles. Between them, and sometimes indeed during them, Arran variously attempts to settle on my shoulder, lap, other arm, or just use me as a short cut, constantly passing over me on a wide circuit of the drawing room. If he can get me to himself, with deafening purr, he kisses me on the ear.

They may settle as a preliminary to waking up for their evening romp. All the energy saved during their sleepy day is released as they, singly or together in about equal proportions, perform acrobatic feats, hide and reappear at surprising angles. This is their kitten hour, which continues when we start preparing for bed. They chase each other upstairs, hide themselves in Sheila's study, or invisibly silent close to us, so much 'not there' that they cannot even find each other. Though there is a long night ahead of them, they are anxious to get to the kitchen to ensure they are fed, but often acrobatics continue till long after we have left. From the bathroom window we can see them at it in their cage, racing up and down the long pole to their 'penthouse'. Except when it is cold, we frequently see them outside should we get up in the middle of the night.

Did I say typical day? All cat lovers know that there is no such thing. The arrival of visitors brings a joyous break in routine. The local black cat might pay one of his periodic visits, sitting like a king on top of their run. As he has matured, Arran has become extremely territorial, and it might now be difficult to introduce a dog or other cat. While Skye sees the black boy as good company, Arran furiously spits and tries to frighten him off. Yet he is always the first to be alarmed by the unexpected: a low-flying aircraft, explosion or even a visit by a previously unseen cat has him rushing in, his tail bushed.

Like all cats, they hate seeing us pack luggage. Skye is particularly dejected when she knows we are ready to go. Yet, if they are spending a night or two at the cattery, she readily jumps into her cage and takes it all in her stride, while Arran resists — and loses weight till he's back home. Which is why, when they can, two members of staff kindly take it in turns to pay an evening visit for cuddle, play and food. The cats frequently visit the office for company when we are absent, terrorising the staff as they dislodge books from the higher-most shelves or disappear into the depths of a large walk-in cupboard.

Despite always having to be sick on a fabric (never the lino) and wasting much of their food, being on the wrong side of doors and especially wanting our attention when it is least convenient, they make us laugh and bring the home to life.

'Jolly expensive,' says Sheila as she puts out their carefully selected food wondering which they will deign to eat tonight.

She may not quite admit it, but good value too.

Chapter 10

CAT WATCHING

It was Hugh Gaitskell, former leader of the UK's Labour Party, who listed girl watching among his hobbies. That girls have their attractions few men would disagree; one naturalist's delight in studying younger ones is quoted on page 219. If nobody has yet formally acknowledged cat watching as a hobby, it is because looking at them is seen as an intrinsic part of caring for the beasts. Conversely, we can be cat lovers in a way that few would publicly admit to being girl lovers.

On a walk I considered the difference between the joys of girl and cat watching. While willingly conceding that certain members of the opposite sex of our own species have a unique, sometimes irresistible attraction, in the lists I concocted in my head walking along the promenade, cats won handsomely. Girls in fact were shameful losers. If a single word sums up the cats' advantage it must be wholesomeness. Consider the following.

Cats of all ages are natural. While they are undoubtedly hedonist attention seekers, they don't smear their faces with make-up, or seductively expose selected curves. They don't smoke, and examples of their drinking alcohol are rare curiosities usually caused by human folly. Never pretending to be older or younger than they are, cats naturally go through their life cycle from frisky kittenhood to middle-age spread (usually of a minor sort) to somnolent old age; few let themselves go as do many older women who have given up caring for their figure, clothing or hair. Cats scrupulously groom themselves throughout their lives.

Then, while we might be dismissed as eccentric crouching to converse with a moggie, there is no threat to the loyalty of our human partner. And if a moggie disdains us, it is no great thing either — while even smiling at a girl can result in an insulting snub, or possibly lead to things better not done. While nobody could claim that when a female cat comes on heat her sex life is exactly pretty, it is for a limited prescribed time. Happily there is no feline equivalent to the heavily made-up, scantily clad girls going out clubbing on a Friday night with the obvious intention of getting drunk or bedded. In short, cats aren't vulgar.

It is perhaps in the simple act of walking that cats demonstrate their superiority. I never grow tired of watching their movements. They can be in a determined hurry, progressing more or less in a straight line with minimum disruption for scratching. Creatively, they are usually more self-questioning, discovering fascinating objects and smells as they cautiously approach you or stalk a mouse, leaving themselves a perfectly rational exit ploy should they not think it appropriate to get close to you, or should something disturb the mouse. 'I never intended to,' is spoke large if they purposefully deviate down what we are supposed to believe was all along going to be their chosen route. They save face with natural grace and style, their paws and minds, all the parts of their complicated bodies in unison.

Two black cats live in the same house in a lane down which I pass just often enough for them to remember me. If I call a greeting, each is anxious for me to stroke it first, but of course does not want either me or the other one to know. They parallel each other in a series of choreographed leaps, delays, diversions, little jumps forward and – for the winner – the most natural tumble which happens to expose the tummy a couple of inches beyond my reach. One then welcomes me crouching forward to stroke its undercarriage; the other likes me to try but takes exception to my succeeding and dashes off. The trouble is that they are so alike that I cannot readily tell which is which. No matter: the pleasure is in watching their tactical approach, accompanied by an occasional meow in answer to my chatter.

Suppose girls acted like that, you might ask. It is not a fair question; you would hardly expect a girl to walk on four limbs any more than a cat to do so upright. But while cats cunningly beguile us, or express sheer indifference, they do it in the time-honoured way common to most of the species. A combination of motor transport and the fashion industry has spoilt the ability of millions of women to put one foot in front of the other in a God-given manner. As humans have become more obsessed with appearance and topical fashion, cats look and certainly behave unchanged. It is like the difference between eating a meal full of fat, salt and additives at a noisy restaurant and enjoying wholesome plain fresh food at home.

Not that cats are unaffected by human fashion. While I love Orientals, the extreme narrowness of many of their heads has a definite downside, in the case of Siamese so much so that there is now a recognised 'traditional' breed.

When it comes to other people's cats in the great outdoors, moggies nearly always seem to be more enjoyably watchable. They show a special gift for being simultaneously cautious and confident.

Except on roads, cats rarely get themselves into trouble, for each move is considered carefully. Prowling around, they clearly own their territory with superior knowledge of nooks and crannies, their memorised 'map' strengthened by hundreds of smells. While their sense of smell is unbeatable and they also use their sense of touch through their paws as well as whiskers, don't underestimate how much they navigate by sight ... or the enjoyment they in turn receive from how they find their way, checking on the familiar and finding something slightly different, as well as noticing a vast range of movement of things animate and inanimate. Everything that moves, including humans, concerns them.

The cat up a post patiently observing a mouse or shrew in the undergrowth beneath will still register the passage of a man or woman (and notice which) a quarter of a mile away. He will decide whether you are approaching near enough or not to impose on his immediate plans. If you get nearer, his body language will reveal his feelings – particularly if he sees you as potential friend or troublemaker. In the latter case, he may become so uneasy that he has to retreat from his vantage point and so probably lose the mouse he had under surveillance. Rarely indeed does he use his voice on first recognition, though as you get close he may answer a greeting or – out of sheer delight – acknowledge that you have taken the trouble to visit him.

Even then, the angle of his tail reveals more: a gentle wagging denoting uncertainty, an upright one positive anticipation, and one bushed out like a brush, fright or even anger. We will return to body and vocal communication later in the chapter.

For many of us, the best cat watching is when we remain unseen or become so much a fixture in the landscape that we don't prevent their deeply channelled concentration into what immediately concerns or pleases them. A prime example is when the wind blows autumn leaves. Kittens and young cats are equally adept at dancing with them, jumping over them, pouncing on selected ones, suddenly grasping whole bunches blowing up within their reach, one leaf or many giving instant but quickly replaced pleasure. Our human equivalent would have been when we were young and, perhaps enjoying a sloping sunlit field, charging around as March hares though, unlike cats, usually with contact with our family, or friends of similar age. Freedom. Freedom of a kind adults seldom experience.

Freedom in cat terms means making the most of the whole environment. Single leaves, leaves blown in heaps, are chased or pounced upon with ecstasy that often becomes so powerful that for good measure they have to dart up a tree or take a rapid arc round our ankles before chasing a leaf again becomes pressingly vital. On such occasions cats must think they are the very wind itself. The kitten in cats often persists for a far greater proportion of their lives than the child in us; ponder that point.

Until she was at least ten, and in human terms well into middle or even retirement age, my Siamese Sara loved sunny, windy spring days when she could partner bunches of daffodils being blown around. 'Weaving through a yellow bed as if she herself were the revolving wind,' as my son

Gareth put it in his memory of Sara on page 116. Delightful though that was, it has to be said that, ever the show-off, Sara performed best when she knew we were watching her. Siamese make perfect pets, and bond so strongly with their humans that they are always involved with them when together, which (including sleeping) is much of the time. They are also wonderful to watch (if we can get near enough without our presence being realised) as they hunt alone perfectly naturally, though even then I suspect are in part driven by the desire to bring us a juicy, bloody present.

Though many of them also value being part of a family, most moggies more easily lose themselves in rapturous natural delight, and are less likely to discover or be influenced by our presence. The wilder the cat, possibly the greater the pleasure he derives from something as basic as autumn leaves blowing about. But then, the young in many species are superb acrobats; it is part of their training for self-survival. Part of the magic of the wild ecstasy displayed by cats interacting with the blown leaves or daffodils is that they dart about too quickly for even the most skilful cameraman to capture sequences in close-up. Nothing we come across close to home is more natural, or in the best sense wilder, than a cat prancing and pouncing this way and that, with impromptu vertical leaps and dashes off stage. It is so hard to film such fast and unexpected movements that, long ago, I decided it was better to enjoy the real thing with the naked eye.

Television shows us all kinds of wild creatures, hunting, fighting, courting, bringing up their young, but because of their fast and erratic movements, few cats make movie stardom in the way that, for example, penguins do. Penguins are good on film because they are so totally uninhibited, ignoring a photographer and his camera, and move in what seems to us a very comic way. Penguins, however, don't live with us. Alone among wild things, only cats inhabit our homes and our lives. That is the difference: the sophisticated hunting machine is the same animal who craves our love and purrs on our lap.

We are all good at seeing what particularly attracts us. Out in the country, some people will note an early or abundant corn crop, a rare flower, an ancient farmhouse or – where most people would assume there are no railways – a signal or even a train. Cat lovers naturally spot more cats than others; it is a skill that grows with experience. Even from lanes in which a cat is rarely seen we might spot one walking along the skyline in distant fields, fascinated by a movement in the undergrowth by the side of a brook, sitting on a gatepost or – occasionally – dancing around in sheer delight. If we have the time, it is usually worth stopping, remaining unspotted or at least uninvolved.

I recall episodes of intense pleasure from seeing cats patrol their territory and behave in a one-off way never to be seen again. One such example especially comes to mind. It was watched from the comfort of our Devon farmhouse. Each spring the new season's lambs spent a period in the field immediately across the lane in front of us. They amused us as they competed to occupy a small platform of turf that, for a reason long lost in agricultural history, had been created several feet above the level of the surrounding land. In what we nicknamed King of the Castle, three or four frisky lambs would climb onto the elevated piece, immediately followed by others who wanted their turn and who deliberately or accidentally squeezed off those already on the eminence, only for them to try to push their way up again. The constant jostling in play of the lambs, plus the occasional dash of a hare around the field's edge, spelt March, spring fever, expectation.

One year, however, I noticed that a tabby, not seen by us before and presumably from the nearby village, had climbed onto a small decaying branch of what remained of a dying tree at the edge of the raised area. It seemed to enjoy the antics of the lambs as much as we did, and probably, like us, also noticed that when the mum sheep below called, all the lambs darted down without hesitation to feed at the right teats. To my amazement, however, just once I saw the tabby actually join in King of the Castle and, when space became scarce as the raised ground was crowded with jostling lambs, neatly jump over the head of one of them to regain its perch.

As cats readily demonstrate when contemplating a mouse or vole, the essence of nature watching is patience. But for us it is not a narrowly specialised occupation, for we can also revel in the beauty of nature, the joy of the open air and stimulating pleasurable thoughts. Indeed, who deliberately goes out to look for cats? The thing is to be cat aware and ready to make the most of opportunities.

Cat watching in towns is more frequently a matter of whether or not cat and human want to make friends. Town cats are more used to contact and understand better which human will suit their mood of the moment. In an unfamiliar place, we can be surprised by how few cats show any interest in us at all, or on another occasion how many follow us or demand to be let in through their front door.

Cats excel at simultaneously showing their independence

and making humans serve their needs. The latter, especially out in the streets, has nothing to do with food. The Siamese, or more likely a moggie, chirping as he follows his human is needing company, emotional support … or maybe access to the warmth of indoor living. Some cats obviously think that they have been snubbed if we cannot respond to their plea to open their own front door. What, after all, are humans for? On a cold day, I once saw a girl of eight or nine ring a doorbell to tell the master of the house that his cat needed letting in. Since the man was on a telephone call, the interruption didn't go down too well, though – as the girl smilingly pointed out to me – the cat nipped in anyway.

What we do not always know is whether a cat is on the doorstep of its established home or out visiting or planning to move; even shooing away doesn't necessarily prove whether or not it belongs there. Over the years I have watched a couple of interesting progressions.

In the first, a small and very ordinary black cat which I had frequently seen on the doorstep and in the window of a cottage on one side of a village street started fraternising with a rather superior pair of grey cats, whom I took to be siblings, in the grounds of a house on the opposite side, though a few doors down. The greys, who had seemed very content with their own company, were apparently enchanted by the small black one, little more than half their size. One day I saw a woman carry the black cat back to its proper home. It didn't seem very pleased. Cats prefer to make or cancel their own social arrangements. Next day, and in the end every day, the black was back with the greys, an unusually happy trio for seldom do siblings welcome a third party. Passing a few days later, I noticed that when the door was opened, all three walked in, though the black was put back outside. But it had decided – that was to be its home. Who knows what thought processes, indeed what benefits, moving across the street would confer. But move it did.

In the other case, I saw a woman looking guilty as she put out a handsome tortoiseshell. 'It's not my cat; it just likes to spend time here,' she explained as I passed. It was not long before it was her cat. Something had prompted it to change homes and make the humans comply with its wish.

The best of all cat watching is at home where we are in close proximity to our cat(s) and have ample time to study their behaviour and reaction. As Jack Richter puts it in his *Your Talking Cat*, having a cat is like having a permanent seat in the front row of a pantomime. 'When you watch a cat, you are watching the embodiment of a natural writer, a gifted actor and singer, a director and producer – all in one kinetic package.' Such entertainment comes for the price of a tin or pouch of cat food and a few scratches on the furniture.

As I write this on a sunny spring morning, Arran has dashed into my study as though chased by the devil, talking endlessly at the top of his voice while positively hitting me with his bushy tail. It was his choice to stay outside and enjoy the sun, but oh, the pent-up desire to make friends has resulted in sheer theatre. Watching his body movements as he steadily becomes less agitated sure beats anything I have seen on TV this week. But I have to respond and watch closely to get the full value from it. Now, reassured we still have each other, he's crawled over Skye to fall asleep in an igloo made for one. He'll stay there till lunch unless the doorbell rings when he'll shoot out, pummelling Skye in the process, to see who's arrived.

As with any entertainment, you do need to pay attention. Owners perhaps most enjoy playing with or having other physical contact with their cat, or watching their antics when they play alone or with another cat. However, just looking at your cat even when it doesn't romp about can be extremely satisfying and help you to understand it. The time I find it especially hard not to laugh is when a cat is too lazy to get up but has its curiosity aroused. Throw a crumpled piece of paper at or near a cat and it can maintain a look of utter astonishment for one to two minutes. It stays still yet eyes the paper, possibly wondering if it might move. It is the same look of concentration given to a moving pen or ruler, whether or not it is dabbed at or chased.

Though experts agree we still have more to discover, we can appreciate the many ways in which cats make their mood and needs known to each other and to humans. Many children in particular start by thinking that purring denotes happiness, wagging of the tail the opposite. The reality is more sophisticated and all the variations of purr and tail are still only two of the many ingredients of body language. As we get to know our cats better we learn that meowing is also a much more complex subject than we at first believed. There are perhaps two ideal starting points.

One: realise that a cat is a cat, essentially caring for its own needs but also a great exhibitionist, delighting in showing her (let the feminine sex have a turn) feelings and prepared to go to extreme lengths to be appreciated for the individualist and comedian she is. Undoubtedly she loves her humans, though often one of them especially, and is sincere in that love though, as has been mentioned earlier, cat and human have not yet lived long enough together for the cat to be able to tell us fully how much she loves us. Though she nuzzles us with her head, purrs on our lap, and is undoubtedly concerned for our welfare (and not just because if she loses us she will need to find a replacement and possibly less-compliant human), sufficiently showing us how deeply she loves is the one thing she finds frustratingly difficult. Otherwise the healthy cat is free from the psychological hang-ups most of our own race suffers. If only we could kick off, work out our feelings … and forget.

Two: cats are great observers of their owners, generally studying us more than we do them. While they do not like being stared at or made to feel self-conscious, they do not ignore us and don't like us ignoring them. The powers of observation of the cat outdoors have already been stressed. She is no less alert inside, feet away from us. She looks and looks, and, as Konrad Lorenz put it, 'few animals display their mood via facial expressions as distinctly as the cat'.

Yet so powerful are her antennae that she can understand us perfectly well even if she becomes blind. She feels us and our movements. She hears us and the sounds we and our artefacts make; for example, readily distinguishing between the different engine tones of a family's several cars. She knows the sounds of different doors and drawers being opened and closed. Test the awareness of your cat by seeing how quickly she realises that treats are now kept in a different cupboard or container. When hearing our footsteps, she instantly knows if we are coming her way or going upstairs or to our kitchen. If there is more than one dog, her sense of smell will tell her which.

She is an expert at sensing mood. Sometimes cats are called telepathic. Usually, however, there is an explanation for their knowing what we don't. For example, it is now realised that cats who warn of a forthcoming earthquake have picked up advance mini-tremors through the sensitive pads on their paws. If our cat fails to greet us on our return, or slinks off into isolation before the front door is opened, it is because she might have heard unhappy conversation as we got out of the car or even remembered an unresolved argument from earlier in the day or preceding night.

Cats intensely dislike being shouted at; their psyche simply cannot take it without a period of recovery. Look at how a shouted-at cat stays out of harm's way. 'Sulking', we humans too readily assume. If we did the same thing, we might be sulking, but the cat is not. She might well understand why you had to shout – possibly because the fire in front of which she was sleeping had starting spitting. See how she steadily recovers, bearing no malice, though anxious to avoid having to be shouted at again too soon. An hour or two on, even if a lesson has been learnt, the hurt is forgotten.

The more you study how cats behave and the better you get to know them, the more you realise that their powers of understanding are enormous. Through their great patience, they have ample time to test cause and effect and sharpen their knowledge. Only rarely are they psychic; they just put it all together. They understand far more than their nature means they have to or it is convenient to reveal. They just like to know all they can about us, though the depth to which that goes obviously varies between cats. Thus Skye keeps a much sharper eye on me (and for that matter on Arran) than he does – not that he is by any means unaware of how we can help him enjoy a richer and more luxurious life, which naturally involves him telling us how much he regards us and, when appropriate, needs our company. If you want to know and understand your cat better, spend longer studying her in all her moods and try to piece cause and effect together. Above all try, and enjoy, watching all the means she employs to communicate, with humans or other cats, or for that matter dogs or hamsters. In doing this, the great realisation is how brilliantly co-ordinated are her various means of staying in touch. For example, though tail angles can tell us much, they are seldom the whole story. When cats answer us back, or have something they want to raise with us, their meow – though that in itself has a greater range than most cat owners realise – needs to be read with their body language. It is not complicated ... infinitely less demanding than doing the crossword or solving the day's Sudoku. But we do need to start with a clean slate, erasing pre-conceived notions, including things we might have been incorrectly taught when young. That is the problem.

The fun thing is that individual cats deploy their communication skills in differing ways that go on evolving. Cats are capable of extending their complex repertoire of tricks throughout their life. My Sara developed extra varieties of vocal messages well after she had turned twenty. And, as for our own education, once you gain a better handle on how your own cat communicates its desires, you will enjoy learning more, since after living with a pet for years it is still possible suddenly to realise what a specific posture or voice denotes.

It took me a long time to distinguish between two of Skye's meows. At first I could not tell the difference though eventually, through careful listening, I detected a slight variation. Both are used when standing on our tall fridge just inside the kitchen door, where she often awaits our arrival no doubt wondering what benefit she can get from us. The first meow is undoubtedly a greeting, expressing the hope I'll let her out or pick her up and spend time with her. She stands alert, upright, expectant. Naturally enough, if at first I ignore her – however much you love a cat, there are occasionally other priorities – she reiterates her call louder and longer until, surprise, it is more comfortable for me to give her my attention than to complete what I was doing. That is why cat lovers often leave a trail of half-completed tasks.

Sometimes, however, I come into the kitchen simply to collect my raincoat and go out for a walk. This is not first thing in the morning, for I wouldn't be so cruel as to ignore Skye then, but later when she again happens to be waiting expectantly on the fridge. I had long heard her meows but deliberately avoided looking at her. When I eventually did, however, I saw the very similar meow being uttered with her face pointing to the ceiling, her whole body sadly limp and ceasing to express hope. Her meow to the ceiling was one of disappointment. 'Oh be like that; just don't expect me to attend to you just when it is convenient for you.' Which of course is just the sentiment many cat lovers express about their pet when she is being 'silly'. If I go to stroke her on my way out of the house, she is only mildly receptive and eyes me in a way that conveys I'm a complete let-down. On Sunday mornings her just seeing the church collection envelope is enough to make her limp since she knows we are going out for a long time and there will be no morning work session in my study.

The cat lover's openness to knowing their cat is key to mutual happiness. Nothing replaces observation, and those who rely heavily on formal learning will probably never attain the enjoyment of real understanding. However, running through a few elementary pointers may help.

Though most communication is by other methods, it is natural to start with voice. Some cats make little audible noise; others use a 'silent' meow for specific purposes. A long time ago, Charles Darwin, of the *Origin of Species*, suggested that 'under various emotions and desires' at least six or seven different vocal sounds were distinguishable. Recent research suggests that up to a score of variations are audible to humans, though perhaps four times as many are not within the range of our hearing.

Because cats' hearing is higher pitched than ours, we can often achieve the best response by making a squeaky sound. That cats also make an effort to adjust to us is suggested by their generally speaking more deliberately to us than among themselves. How many meows can you identify in your cat? For instance, does she use a special short response if simply acknowledging that she is in conversation with you? If you continue to greet some cats a dozen or more times, they continue making their short acknowledgement which says no more than 'Yes, we're in contact'. And does your cat growl, hiss, yodel or chatter? Guttural chattering or chittering often expresses the sheer frustration of not being able to get at prey outside their reach, such as birds trespassing on the window ledge ... those winged mice and rats who cheat by flying.

A cat whom we found particularly explicit in his speech was a chocolate-point Birman, with long fur making him look larger than he felt, at a hotel in Penzance, Cornwall. When we walked through the front door, he was prettily sitting on the reception desk and gave us what was clearly an introductory greeting.

The receptionist then said, 'Welcome,' but since he had already said that and didn't like being upstaged, he made it clear that it was he who was welcoming us.

I enquired what he was called.

'Thomas.'

'Yes, that's me,' meowed Thomas. And when I spoke his name he entered into a long piece of gentle but fairly continuous conversation. There was a further, slightly sharper, greeting when I started stroking him.

'You can have him if you want,' said the receptionist. 'He has far too much to say for himself. By the way, could I have your name?'

'Thomas.'

'Really! You should certainly have him. You're made for each other.'

Thomas was inclined to agree, and when we walked off to our bedroom uttered an abrupt short meow: 'Where do you think you're going?'

He was not slow to appear when we came back down for a cup of tea by the fire. Another greeting. More continuous conversation. When I picked him up, another sharper greeting. And when I stopped stroking him, another abrupt short meow: 'Why are you stopping?' In fact, I deliberately started and stopped stroking about once a minute, and his meowing cycle was repeated exactly.

This pattern was maintained throughout our stay, including in the dining room into which he slipped to hide under our table – but was seen by a waiter whom he condemned with an even more abrupt short meow. It indeed seemed a waste to terminate his enthusiastic mutterings. Next morning, when we paid our bill, Thomas seemed to cry, 'Why does this always happen to me?'

Four very distinguishable meows; I'm sure further study would have revealed others.

The frequency and intensity of purring is almost as varied between cats as the use of their voices. Just approaching some cats who have bonded closely with their human will start them purring, though too sleepy or lazy to get up. 'Yes, I'm glad you have come to see me.' A cat who doesn't purr when ordinary food is presented or discovered may well do so at the pleasure of being offered a treat. Prestige increases happiness. Cats who like to jump onto their owners may start purring in expectation as they calculate the distance to shoulder or arm. Most cats have their engines running fastest when in their favourite cuddling position, gentle extra pressure around the tummy often spurring fresh enthusiasm.

It is fascinating that domestic cats mainly purr when in contact with their owners, while big cats such as lions purr among each other and when enjoying their food. Purring is a form of vibration, said by some to help heal bones and muscles. Some cats respond to other kinds of vibration. An example is Kya whose owner says she takes little notice of an electric organ being played until it is switched to church organ mode. Then she excitedly enjoys the vibration by walking up and down the keys.

The first clue to understanding the importance of body language is to note the cat's stance as it talks to you and purrs. So what would be the most perfect cat? One that greeted us and purred, held a front paw up in expectation, came and rubbed its head and tail against us, eyes semi-closed and blinking, its ears and tail upright, its body and fur relaxed.

Ears reveal a lot. They are upright when things are well, horizontal when the cat is under pressure, and point downward in anger – the more so the greater the unhappiness and threat. Eyes also give a clear signal. Narrowly open and blinking usually means 'I am at ease', fully open that 'I'm trying to find out what it's all about', dilated that there's anxiety or anger. The straight-up tail suggests 'This is going to be all right', the slightly curved raised one goes with 'I'm trying to find out what it's all about', a gently waving one 'I'm trying to make up my mind', and of course a furiously waving or a fully bushed out one accompanied by hissing or growling that there is anxiety or downright anger.

However, cats differ greatly. For example, Skye has her eyes fully open far more of the time than any other cat I have known. When she purrs at full pelt, not only does she often have her eyes fully open staring at me, but she also seems to enjoy my looking back at her with only occasional blinks. Added to that her ears are bent back. It adds up to what experts see as unhappy, a threatened or threatening cat.

For a long time her appearance made me feel slightly at risk. While she was obviously happy, I feared that perhaps it was too much for her to take emotionally and that she might suddenly spit at me and scratch. Not so. Even in fun she has never once scratched me. We just need to know our own cat, to be able fully to relax as much as to be aware of danger.

While I was writing the last paragraph, Skye rubbed her head and tail against my leg and brushed the typewriter with her head, using that other means of cat communication: smell.

Her scent glands leave telltale traces which, with our inadequate human apparatus, I cannot smell. She undoubtedly goes to bed aware of my scent on her. That such different creatures can so closely relate through these complex ways is perhaps what some people translate as being telepathic. As already said, usually, if we can fathom it, there is a rational explanation. Yet how do cats know when the owner they love is in the operating theatre, dying or dead? Some mystery is not explainable, and perhaps never will be.

Finally, a word to those who have neither the time nor inclination for the closest kind of relationship with a cat. While most cats need at least some interaction with humans, not only does each individual's requirements vary markedly but they will rarely remain the same indefinitely. Making the most of an 'independent' cat when it drops in for its friendly ritual may well mean it stays longer and visits more frequently; conversely the arrival of another pet or a baby might lead to intense jealousy, insecurity and problems such as 'marking' (urinating) around the house.

One thing is certain. While we should know our cats as well as possible and always be kindly and reassuring to them, we cannot discipline them or expect them to 'improve' by shouting at them. They will 'wear the trousers' and certainly determine how much time to spend with us and how much alone.

I cannot finish the chapter on cat watching without returning to the question of pets doing social duty at retirement and care homes. As an incidental, a sad tale has just been reported. A friend lost his black-and-white striped Nelson. It emerged that Nelson had taken himself off to a nursing home, where he was having the time of his life being fussed over by one old lady after another. News of his new regime eventually reached the owner, who was overjoyed to regain his companionship: 'But I left a nursing home full of deprived ladies.'

Dropping in on a relative who had suffered a stroke coincided with a volunteer's tabby's weekly therapeutic visit to the nursing home. The mood changed dramatically as all eyes were on the cat whose name some of the elderly muttered. Dreary gloom was now excited expectation. The cat did not have difficulty accepting that she was the centre of attention; tail erect, she proudly walked around with the dignity of a queen acknowledging her subjects. 'It's the same every week,' said a nurse.

One old man, a recluse, who was normally hard to persuade to leave his room, always came down to the communal lounge to greet the cat. It was a privilege to be present at such a vital time and watch the tabby on her rounds. The owner sensibly took a back seat, commenting that she always knew when it was time for the weekly visit because more of the residents smiled or even smartened up their appearance. The tabby obviously recognised many of her regulars. As an outsider she didn't think I warranted attention, though several times she glanced my way and no doubt appreciated my seeing her perform her miracle of cheering up the folk, especially the recluse who twice had her on his lap. Shouldn't more of us offer the therapeutic service of our cats?

Chapter 11

QUESTIONS

This does not set out to be a 'how to' practical book, but one cat lover's comments might stir thoughts, discussion and better understanding – and possibly help readers broaden their advice to novices.

How do I decide on the cat for me?

Whatever else, avoid buying a cat in a pet shop. If you are getting a kitten from a friend try to find out who is the father. Three things are vital: the character of the dad, who determines most of a kitten's character; good human socialisation in the first few weeks, without which it will never make a good pet; and health. Breeders win on all three counts, so it makes sense to go to someone with a proven track record.

Even then you can be caught. A Bengal breeder singled out one male kitten as a possible stud cat. He was not properly socialised so, when the breeder decided to sell him, the new owner had problems. Not used to being handled, and insecure, at the time of writing the cat is a great bully. Handsome as most Bengals are, he gives much pleasure between bouts of making the family's other cat miserable, causing damage and urinating around the house. The owner now faces the typical problem: behaviour is improving slowly but unpredictably, and he is still too difficult to cope with permanently. Will he have to go? The longer the decision is delayed, the more painful it will be saying goodbye.

It is worth spelling out these details to warn others to be on their guard. This is only one example of several problem cats supplied by breeders. So choose your breeder with care. See also my daughter's comments on page 134.

The best breeders socialise all kittens including those they may keep, but the more there are to be handled the less attention each individual kitten will receive. Ideally your breeder would encourage you to visit and handle your kitten before it is old enough to be separated from its mum.

Unless a cat happens to move in on you, don't become an owner on the spur of the moment. That means don't even think about contacting a breeder until you're ready. Ideally your choice should begin by reading a good book and a few issues of a cat magazine, talking to cat owners and perhaps visiting a cat show. Enjoy the prospect of owning one kind of cat even if you end up choosing another. Family discussion, possibly heated argument, will influence the choice.

Ultimately choice is a very personal matter. Many owners of everyday moggies and of different pedigrees will assure you theirs is the most loveable cat in the world, able to perform amazing tricks. The final selection might well depend on whether you enjoy a cat loudly expressing itself or only making the gentlest sound as it tries to communicate. Siamese and other Orientals make great pets, endearing themselves to the whole family, but many do like to make their presence known, charging into a room as though they were conveying world-shattering news and frequently answering you back.

If there are several kittens available at a breeder, let one choose you by being more inquisitive and taking more interest in you than the others. That is usually the easy part!

One other point, especially relevant if you are making your choice well ahead of taking possession: ask the breeder to ensure that the cat is used to noises such as the vacuum cleaner. If not, it might be frightened all its life, as unfortunately is my Arran. He thinks the vacuum is the very devil.

Wouldn't it be kinder to have a rescue cat?

While humans may boast that we have become more civilised and, for example, in the Western world cats are no longer hunted for their meat and fur, the downside is that there are enormous numbers of feral and uncared-for cats. A family of fifteen inquisitive kittens less than a month old was recently abandoned in a street in Chart Sutton, Kent, England; the third such dumping reported in the area to the RSPCA in a week. Added to that, many household cats need re-homing because of family problems and death or, in some cases, because the cat has become too difficult to control.

It is therefore not surprising that nearly one in three owners get their moggies from a charitable rescue operation, the best-known UK examples of which are Cats Protection, the RSPCA and Battersea Dogs & Cats Home, though there are also many smaller regional ones. Between them, almost every minute of the day they save an unwanted cat from having to be put down. In the world as a whole it might be a cat saved every second. In Australia, for instance, though run on a shoestring, the Cat Protection Society of New South Wales finds new homes for nearly a thousand kittens and 400 adults a year. Each transaction is of great importance not only for the cat (who usually shows love and appreciation for being chosen) but also the acquiring family. Sad indeed are the staff when they see a disabled or older cat anxious to be picked up and cherished constantly passed by.

It must, however, be said that choosing a cat with its character fully established, and its ways less mouldable, involves some risk. While the re-homing success rate is high, not all unhappy cats are able to put problems behind them. One who has been maltreated may always be nervous and flinch when someone strokes it. If you are seriously considering a rescue cat, try not to be rushed. If possible, get to know it, in its various moods and at different times of day.

Older people (who account for an increasing proportion of re-homings) may feel it too challenging to start with a kitten, or that it would be selfish to do so since they might not be there to look after it through its lifespan. However, 'It wouldn't be fair to the cat,' probably includes a degree of personal selfishness: 'Nobody else could possibly make my cat as happy as it has been with me.' Which isn't always true, and certainly not if there is a cat-loving relative or friend in the offing. A transfer to a friend or relative who already knows the cat, especially if they have looked after the cat during the owner's absences, greatly reduces the risk.

As with everything else to do with cats, there are always one-offs. Even a pair of blind feral cats gave lasting pleasure to one caring owner. Personal taste and time –

how available and patient are you? – obviously come into your choice. But unless a cat makes decisions for you, do consider your options.

Don't let age too quickly put you off having a cat, for it will do more to keep you fit and alert than any medicine. These days many people are in their seventies before discovering their inner kitten.

How many cats should I have?

Not, please, the 30 (plus various other animals) of a woman advertising for romance with a like-minded male in the personal column of a recent cat magazine. The mind boggles.

If you live on your own, a single cat will undoubtedly bond more closely and give greater pleasure. If you are out for long hours, or take frequent holidays, two cats – if carefully chosen – give each other much support. Try to get siblings, used to each other from the start and unlikely to become sudden enemies, though even that can happen. Coincidentally the latest example of a problem cat to come to my notice – one of two sisters in a household of four cats – is a Bengal. As she matured she took against her sister, though not the other two non-Bengal cats. She fights and chases her sibling enemy and again urinates around the house. Bengals are powerful cats, delightful but not for the faint-hearted even when things go well.

Beyond two cats you enter the realms of risk and uncertainty. Introducing a kitten might stimulate new interest in a pair of older cats ... or cause universal misery. The greater the number of cats the higher the risk of trouble. We have friends with six, all of whom they love, though the cats spend most of their time outside except at night when they sleep in two sets of three-tiered beds. Significantly, most of them sleep by themselves, though usually siblings and often other pairs will cuddle together throughout life. Our friends are real cat lovers, responsible, considerate and energetic people who have achieved more for their pets than would most. They greatly enjoy the cats around them, exploring or working in the garden and, one of them especially, coming into the house to meet visitors. Yet even they perhaps lack the joy of closely bonding with an individual cat who is with you many hours a day.

Ernest Hemingway – 'one cat just leads to another' – had 30 cats, at his famous house on a hilltop in Havana. He loved their 'absolute emotional honesty' and no doubt gave them all the comfort and attention he could; yet generally more cats does not spell happiness any more than does monetary wealth. (My Australian editor interjects that when her parents lived on a farm just outside Thame, Oxfordshire, her mother had 24 cats, although only twelve of them came inside. She herself has just Cola, who sits beside her as she works.)

While several cats might love you, and the attention you give them, cats are naturally jealous of each other. Skye has a malicious expression if Arran is on my lap; Arran has to imitate Skye and land on me when I am cuddling her. Things generally work out because during a typical day each has solo purring time. Much though I enjoy the contrast between them as well as their behaviour together, there is no doubt that as a sole cat either one would be even closer to us. But if the only one were Skye, she would pine more desperately when, disloyally, we went on holiday.

Girl or boy?

Writing in a way that few editors would accept today, the naturalist W. H. Hudson extolled the virtues of little girls (usually of six to eight) and his repertoire of bygone memories of 'human flowers who shine and pass out of sight like flowers of the meadow'. Later he explained: 'To go from little girls to little boys is to go into another, an inferior, coarser world.' The female of most species matures sooner, and undoubtedly girl kittens turning into young adults are more precocious and mature, and so better company than their brothers. They are surer footed, more secure in your love, more understanding of how things work. Nature is of course preparing them for the responsibility of early parenthood.

Girl cats always retain female characteristics, such as generally liking men better than women, but being far more interested in woman's dressing and clothing. If I had only one cat, especially if I lived alone, it would be a girl. Yet though they start behind in the race towards intelligence and getting the best out of life, the boys steadily catch up and frequently overtake their sisters. Boys are slower developers, which has its charm as well as irritations. In my experience, in their first couple of years they are great copiers of their sister's tricks, and then become very much their own person, and usually also very loveable and loving though territorially more protective and more likely to cause trouble seeing other cats and animals off so that they have you and where you live to themselves. Certainly, I know of cat lovers who unlike me, feel they can bond more closely with a boy.

My current brother-and-sister cats always act their gender, and again – but this time with special reference to their behaviour as male and female – it is fascinating watching their different reactions and attitudes. They regularly groom each other and spend long hours cuddled tightly together, though sometimes have serious as well as play fights. The female always holds her own and usually gives the impression of being the superior of the partnership even though the boy is the first to lunge on to our laps. Recently I heard of siblings quarrelling over a food bowl; the standard advice is to give each their own. In my experience competing for their owner's attention is far more common than pushing for food. In fact, personally I have only heard of two or three isolated cases of animosity at eating times, though a few more of bullying control by blocking the passage to the cat flap.

What should I call my cat?

In his *Old Possum's Book of Practical Cats*, T. S. Eliot advised that a cat needs a minimum of three names: a family name, a formal one and one only known to the cat itself. Sara thought she was Sara Cat, and Skye and Arran also recognise their species name as readily as their own name. It doesn't matter what we call them formally, for it is what we most repeatedly say when calling or referring to them that they recognise. Eliot would have been tempted to shorten even Macavity if he were calling a cat in on a dark night, holding the door open during a blustery shower. Usually the only time names suggestive of the good things in life are ever fully used is on the forms that come with pedigree cats. No doubt they help justify the steep price demanded for a teeny bundle of fluff.

During our lifetime there has been a tendency to drop human names in favour of those presumably thought to be more cat-like. At least that avoids confusion of the kind experienced when I once stayed with friends. As I was about to drop off to sleep, 'David' was shouted urgently. I rushed to the landing to discover it was also the name of their cat. Increasingly, perhaps, we seek to give our cats more original names – and more original ones than our dogs too. We thought that naming ours after two Scottish islands was original until one day we delivered them to the cattery where the very same cage had just been vacated by another Skye and Arran.

Do names matter? To many people, yes. There is, for example, only one home I know where cats called Auberon and Zambenflöte would have fitted (see page 162). Partly for fun – though do make creative use of it – I have included an index of cats by name. Note how most of the names are obviously chosen more to reflect the character of their owners than the innocent cats. Relatively few sound affectionate, though some are quite good to be shouted at an errant feline. At least do better than an English hotel that had a ginger-and-white stray move in. The staff began calling it Smelly Cat, which unfortunately stuck. Very clean, it isn't the least bit smelly.

Should I take out cat insurance?

Cats may have nine lives but some of them can be costly. Insurance companies play on our emotions, talking of the need for peace of mind. Large sums are spent by the rival companies advertising their very varied products, while administering schemes for the relatively small premiums involved is expensive. So if we took the risk ourselves, on average we would be considerably in pocket. Naturally you are more likely to achieve the average if you spread risk across several things ... not more cats but other kinds of insurance. Houses and cars excepted, most of us realise that if we had the courage to accept risks ourselves, putting aside something like an equivalent amount to the premiums, we would be extraordinarily unlucky not to accumulate a useful nest egg.

As with medical or travel insurance, even if large premiums have been paid over many years, help is limited when you suddenly need it. Examine carefully exactly what each particular insurance offers. Many insurers will not take on older cats and will put up their rates as your cats become older and/or impose excesses and annual limits, most per condition. Comparison is hard, and only experience shows how tight-fisted the insurers are when faced with claims, a particular point of contention being whether a problem is a new condition or an extension of one already claimed against.

Naturally those who do have insurance sometimes make expensive claims well exceeding what they have paid. Flossy, a fourteen-year-old affectionate but independent and overweight tabby, was leading a happy life in Christchurch, England, till one day she came home with the pads of her front right paws seriously cut. Though she was treated, soon her paw hooked up and she could not put it down or straighten it. Things went from bad to worse: four major operations including skin grafts were needed, the last one to amputate totally her front right leg. 'Throughout she's been understanding and affectionate,' says her owner, Clive

Carwardine Palmer, ‘but as well as continually taking her to and from vets, for long periods we have had to watch her closely to prevent her jumping and doing damage. After the first three operations and a skin graft that went wrong, her medical cover was used up. That was a maximum of £4800 but reduced by a quarter to £3600 because of Flossy’s age. So the final amputation has had to be paid for.’ Meanwhile Flossy’s sister, also a fourteen-year-old tabby — ‘an inquisitive scamp’ — has continued to be insured for £7 a month, without any claim being made for her.

‘Since we’ve got back more than we paid in, I suppose we could be called “lucky”. But it hasn’t been perfect, with lots of correspondence and paperwork and arguments about whether the skin graft that went wrong was a new condition — they said it was part of the same problem. The important thing is that Flossy has been loving throughout and now seems perfectly happy with three legs. She’s a treasure.’

Several of the enquiries made for this book coincided with news of another cat tragedy. When I spoke to Clive, he had just returned with his wife Jane from comforting their daughter’s partner (the daughter was away on business) for the loss of one of their pair of sisters in a road accident the previous night. Clive added: ‘At one of our previous homes, realising the traffic at the front was dangerous, we only allowed our two cats out at the back, but Pickle was killed on a little-used lane.’ While writing the book, I must have heard of well over a hundred road deaths ... and one cat killed by a train. Cats Protection says around a million cats are involved in road accidents in the UK every year; they are helping promote a new warning sign showing a cat asking motorists to watch their speed.

Why do my cats prefer my husband?

If many cats, boys as well as girls, feel more secure with men, it is because, with their lower voices, men sound more respectful. Even though cats hear high-pitched sounds the clearest, shrieking and laughing easily deters them. Some women are their own worst enemy in the cat stakes. Once more, it doesn't matter what you say but it must never be capable of being interpreted as ridicule. Men are probably also better at making the best use of the limited words that the cats understand.

Isn't it cruel to keep a cat indoors?

It depends on many factors. Is it cruel to deprive those who could not possibly have an outdoor cat of one altogether? Even a rescue cat needing a home? Anyway, in many places today's fast traffic poses a serious problem. Taking other risks into account (hooliganism, feral and bullying cats, stealing of pedigree cats), many of us have concluded that, on balance, the indoor route is the better if not perfect option.

Skye and Arran would surely enjoy hunting; I would love them to follow me around the garden as did my earlier Sara. They do however live in a largish house, and have a cat flap into a decent run with things to climb and a platform from which they can survey the outside world. As indoor cats go they are perhaps spoilt, though Arran still shows occasional signs of distressing unrest, pacing up and down not knowing what to do with himself. Skye, like the female of most species, knows how to make the best use of her constraints. At least we don't come home anxious to see if they are still alive.

If you are planning on a sole indoor cat, perhaps choose a girl. A pair, ideally siblings, would be better, for they make much more of their own fun, including mock hunting and occasional harmless quarrelling helping to burn up the energy. Always give an inside cat a vantage point or two to make life as varied as you can. All cats watch birds even if they cannot catch them. If you are in a flat with a balcony, can it be made cat tight? Jess, the small friendly, demanding Burmese who features in The Parable of the Cat on page 239, has two: one in which she can soak up the sun, and a lower arbour-like one covered by vegetation.

Finally, do feed the natural curiosity of cats by leaving open a drawer normally closed or tossing an empty box to the floor and trailing a piece of string for them to pounce on. Just before going to bed is the perfect time to help use up spare energy.

Can't I take my cat out on a lead?

Some cats are happy with a collar and lead; occasionally you see them on walks like small dogs. Many kittens are, however, already too fixed in their ways by the time they leave their breeders. Start training as early as possible.

A lead implies a collar, and currently they are getting a bad press with frequent warnings of cats being caught up in an obstruction and damaging themselves in efforts to get free. Many bird lovers only have a cat on condition it has a collar with a bell to give warning of danger. That might still be acceptable if your cat stays within your own garden, but otherwise is risky.

Isn't there another solution?

Yes, but I have only seen it at work once, in the USA, where it is quite common. Cats are allowed into an area (small or of several acres) ringed round by an invisible electric fence buried underground. A device fitted to the collar gives an audible warning when the boundary is being approached, and a small electric shock if it is actually reached. The electric wire is still buried, though more deeply, under driveways so even if a gate is open the cats are still kept in, though marauders could enter.

Training usually begins with a pair of bowls of tuna fish. One, with a flag, gives off a small shock when touched, which it won't be a second time. Outside, similar small flags are laid out around the area encircled by the electric wire, though some say that is an unnecessary complication for the audible warning and electric shock quickly do their own work. The solution is especially welcome in America, where there are few boundary walls or hedges around gardens. And since cats are anyway constrained and can be quickly found if missing, wearing a collar doesn't hurt. (A recent note in a UK cat magazine highlighted a British equivalent to this American system.)

In a delightful part of Vermont, the Green Mountain State, where my publishing house had its branch many years ago, young Jasper, a Siamese, was quick to demonstrate that the business still thrives. He led the tour of barns, some used for the farm, others by the expanded book business, and his extensive outside territory. Naturally he continually stopped to ensure we were following, or came back for a greeting and stroke, before pouncing forward again — but never attempted to cross the boundary safeguarded by the electric fence. An expensive but eminently successful solution.

In its early years Caroline and Ted Robbins ran the business as managers on their farm. Their earlier Siamese, Ying, who sat on my knee during board meetings, was met on page 111. Later the husband-and-wife team bought out the business and made a great success of it. When I telephoned the office for the first time in years, specifically to check on how Jasper's invisible fence works, I was told that Caroline had gone to the vet. An hour later, she called to tell me she had to take Jasper. His mini penis had become blocked earlier and his waterworks rearranged, at first successfully, but he had been unable to pee over the weekend. That is dangerous for a cat. So first thing Monday morning she was waiting for the vet to open. Predictably, knowing cats, Jasper peed on the vet's table.

Why has my cat gone off its favourite food?

Cats need variety in all things – especially food. A single variety of dry food seems acceptable to those who mainly or partly eat it, but vary the rest of the diet and avoid tiring them of their favourite food, which will then be rejected possibly for months to come or (says Sheila) forever. Most owners accept there will be some waste, since rejected wet food rapidly looks disgusting. Cats prefer little and often; those who feed themselves in the wild consume around ten mice per day caught over many hours. However, some say they better regulate their feeding, and are less likely to become obese, if their food is provided once daily than in frequent smaller amounts. If you have more than one cat, take care that a greedy one doesn't wolf more than their fair share – especially since most cats do not finish a meal at a single sitting.

One hears tales of cats 'having' to be given prime this and that, but that is because their owners have given in too readily. Unless they are ill, cats won't starve. Call their bluff! If you give in, they can develop all kinds of foibles, such as 'having' to be fed by hand. Remember that they are attention seekers. Prestige is important. My cats ignore dried food in the kitchen, but as soon as they come to my study request I pour some (the identical kind) into their bowl. They devour it eagerly. Conversely, a treat I sometimes give them, and of which they have tired, is more welcome if proffered by my wife as an exceptional thing. If you are into cat thinking, it is perfectly logical – don't we humans sometimes enjoy out a dish that we avoid at home? Likewise any food stolen – perhaps from unopened packets in the cats' cupboard accidentally left unlocked – is much more tasty. While cats generally learn quickly, 'yours' and 'mine' is a curious unlearnable human concept. Suitable and unsuitable food left on the kitchen counters is tempting and possibly dangerous fun.

Any special feeding dos and don'ts?

Dairy produce is now seen as unsuitable. Most breeders avoid it, so these days kittens arrive unfamiliar with the saucer of milk or cream. Licking out (which might mean putting their paw in and licking it) an occasional cream tub is surely permissible. Fish, especially tinned tuna, should be given in moderation. Do take care with both fish and chicken bones. Most cats benefit from fresh food such as chicken or beef, but cat food not only comes in a convenient range of flavours but also in special formulae for kittens and older pets. Dog food is not suitable. Chocolate is toxic for cats, as is the pollen of lilies. Many cats have died or become seriously ill licking lily pollen off their coats. All cats are meat eaters and, whatever your own preference, putting a cat on a vegetarian diet is extremely risky not to mention unkind.

Another point: cats enjoy tepid food, neither too hot nor cold. I have known many cats who understood they had to wait for hot food to cool – 'Soon' – but never one who appreciated that what came out of the fridge would taste better later.

Finally, though cats can survive for long periods without food, daily water is vital; even the loss of 15 per cent of an animal's liquid is dangerous, potentially fatal. Again some develop foibles, but these might be excusable. The taste of some cities' treated water is not nice; a dripping tap makes it more acceptable.

Should my pet share my food?

My advice is to avoid sharing at table. If cats are shooed off a laid table they generally avoid it even if it is permitted territory between meals. Making a rare exception, providing a tasty morsel on the rug at Sunday lunch adds to variety and panders to prestige.

How do you stop a cat scratching the furniture?

In my experience you don't. Books and articles tell you to provide scratching posts or stations, which some cats will make use of but most scrupulously avoid. Even for 'good' cats, if there are such things, the time comes when it is more fun to run the gauntlet of the owner's anger than soak up more praise for scratching on the right thing. If properly (which means instantly) administered, water spray is a good deterrent, but purposeful cats readily catch onto cause and effect. They lie in wait until your back is turned, perhaps because the telephone rings or there is another distraction, and then have a go at their favoured piece of carpet or upholstery, in our case the main sufferer being our bed's base. By the time you arrive, they are scurrying away with delight, skilfully avoiding the water jet. Such fun that it is worth the risk of an occasional soaking.

The best policy might be to appear not to notice an attack on anything precious but shout abuse when the scratching post or something that doesn't matter is used. This worked well with Sara when she attacked the cork seat of the then brand-new bathroom stool. It didn't save the stool, but made it her automatic choice when (in fun) I chased her and shouted. She enjoyed the attention and maybe her instinct told her to defend herself by sharpening her claws. Shortening claws is said to help, but I have lacked the time and discipline — or is it courage? — to do that.

If you are going to love a cat, and have it love you, an elementary rule is that it and not you will decide its favourite things. Some damage is inevitable. Our worst has been done by Arran, not to upholstery but the front ledge (in front of the upper windows) of our mahogany glass-fronted cabinet. He will walk along it, using claws to prevent falling off.

The luck of the draw – and inherited wickedness – plays a major role. Several members of my staff had cats that routinely climbed (and damagingly swung from) curtains. They had all come from one mother (owned by our London secretary), who trained successive litters to follow her up one edge of the curtains, swing from the very top and come down the other side. People noticing, even photographing, their acrobatics were an obvious incentive. Not that mothers always succeed in making their kittens understand. One mum taught her kitten how to ensure the owners were brought smartly to attention: threaten the goldfish. One naughty boy kitten actually hooked and started eating a fish. Never was a mother cat more angry; the oft-used threat had become worthless.

Christmas is coming; what is the best present I can give my cat?

The gift of involvement. Apart from food and vet's bills, don't waste money on them but let them get into everything: your dressing, washing and showering, post opening and movements around the house. Let them be everywhere ... but especially in the boxes the postman might have been benevolent enough to bring. A replacement box for your nephew's present might cost a pound or so, but think what you save on clockwork toys and other elaborate cat presents that will not give 10 per cent as much pleasure.

Give your cats yourself. The time they waste will more than be repaid by your sleeping better.

Is it really dangerous to have my cat on the car's back window ledge?

Yes, it is dangerous! Even if your cat never moves and you're convinced it won't get under your feet. Traffic speeds have increased dramatically in recent years, yet casualties have been reduced by improved roads and cars, seat belts and better understanding. In a crash, a cat could be hurled forward like a missile, in danger of injuring or even killing a passenger, as well as being killed itself. Alternatively, if a door burst open, your cat could find itself dazed on the highway.

The adaptability of cats was well demonstrated by Psyche, a silver tabby. She was sixteen before being first taken on journeys, always in a cage. On motorways as well as ordinary roads, she scratched to draw attention to the fact she needed the loo. Allowed out into her litter tray she wasted no time and, having finished with typical scratching about, jumped back into her cage. She did this for four years, dying aged twenty.

Of course, cats love to see what's happening around them. I have seen them happily gazing out from a cage safely secured on a car's back ledge or seat.

Should I allow Victor to have kittens?

The question assumes that Victor was acquired as a tom but – surprise – turned out to be a girl. Few cats called Victoria are named after the noble queen.

It used to be thought that female cats led a happier life if they had one litter of kittens before being neutered, but there is no truth in it. While most cats are natural mothers, like humans, some are awful ... especially first time.

Unless you are seriously into breeding, when a raft of different points applies, one problem about having kittens is the choice of mate. These days most responsible cat owners have their toms neutered (or dressed as it is called in some places), which means that toms on the roam tend to belong to less responsible people or be living in the wild – not the kind of mate you'd ideally choose for your loved one.

If as a non-specialist breeder you seriously want the challenge, make sure you will be around at the appropriate time and that there will be no problems in finding homes for the kittens. Also be prepared for the emotional pull: even if you don't, someone in the family will plead to keep one of them. And do handle the kittens early and regularly or they will never socialise with humans properly. Happily most mums (or 'queens') delight in their offspring being picked up and admired.

How long will my cat live?

In the Western world, like humans, cats have never had it better or lived longer. According to Whiskas, half of UK cats are 'seniors', which they say is eight years or older – surely too young an age? Whiskas say that, at the time of writing, Britain's oldest cat is Whisky, age 34, which they equate to 149 in cat years. That, however, is only about four and a half cat years to one human one, whereas the lives of cats and dogs have traditionally been multiplied by seven to give human equivalents. Yet if you multiply 34 by seven it produces an even more ridiculous human equivalent of 238.

Times seven to give a cat a human age equivalent doesn't work as well as it used to, not only because feline life expectancy has increased even faster than that of humans, but also because more individual cats (certainly more than dogs) well outlive the average. And though pockets of poverty still reduce the average UK human lifespan, in the feline world there is a dramatic contrast between feral cats (lone ferals may be lucky to reach their third birthday) and pampered pets. Few humans reach 110, while many Siamese happily go on well into their twenties. Better food and heating is one reason; another is the rising proportion of cats that receive vet care, and the great increase in feline medical knowledge and skill. As we saw earlier, that was rudimentary as late as the 1950s.

Though there are also more active days, cats (like humans) tend to spend an increasing proportion of life in contemplative retirement. Because, in Britain at least, cats are outside the law, there is little official data. Estimates vary, but well over half of all cats are thought to reach twelve or over, with an average lifespan of sixteen. Yet nine (which times seven gives a human equivalent of 63) is the age when most cats seem to begin to slow down and are entitled to the equivalent of our free bus pass. Older cats spend three-quarters of their time sleeping, but usually make excellent use of the other quarter. Though they become more home based, the hunting instinct remains strong till the end. If those living in sheltered accommodation can only chase an insect, they still do it with artful cunning.

Though all become more susceptible to problems, including heart, the older they are, a large proportion of cats die of fewer causes than do humans. In real old age kidney failure is a common cause of cats losing their dignity and having to be put to sleep. There is not much we can do about that, but in many other ways owners can help extend their cats' lives. Microchipping helps restore many to their homes. Awareness of traffic problems, and checking the cat isn't in danger when starting up the car in the drive, saves lives, though it is hard to train cats not to make a dangerous dash for it across a busy road or, in many cases, not sit in the middle of a highway.

As cats age, their sense of taste decreases, so greater variety is called for in the feeding bowl. Digestive abilities wane, so older cats need to eat more; special foods are available to help. Digestion is also hurt by poor oral health. Having the vet routinely check mouths is important; poor teeth often mean it is hard to bite dry food and so pouch and canned varieties come to the rescue. There is much we can do to extend our cat's lives – above all by pandering to their natural curiosity.

Several books include a table of cats' ages and human equivalents. Mine is shown on the following page. It shows kittens developing faster than others suggest, having a longer adulthood and middle age, with equivalent human years again passing faster in old age. The table accords with my own experience in recent years; it would have looked quite different a human generation ago. It is based on well-cared-for domestic cats. Those living in the wild have far shorter lives. And because cats are such individualists, averages are more subject to dramatic variations than with humans.

CAT AGE	HUMAN EQUIVALENT AGE
10 weeks	8 years
7 months	14 years
1 year	18 years
2 years	25 years
4 years	33 years
6 years	40 years
8 years	50 years
10 years	60 years
12 years	65 years
14 years	70 years
16 years	80 years
18 years	84 years
20 years	88 years
21 years	92 years

THE FINAL WORD

I would like to end with the following story from Sheila McCullagh, first published in the *Bath Abbey News*.

THE PARABLE OF THE CAT

I have often found praying difficult to understand, especially when prayers seem to go unanswered, no matter what the need; but a very simple happening at home last Monday has helped me. It concerned our kitten, Jess. Jess is six months old. She trusts us completely to provide her with food and TLC whenever she asks (which is very often). On Monday, she was spayed. She had been out on Sunday with us in the car (she lives in a flat and likes to go out, especially if there are pigeons to watch), but when she came back she was too tired to eat much supper. We tried hard to coax her, but to no avail. Consequently, in the morning she was longing for breakfast, which is her main meal of the day. But of course I couldn't give it to her, because she was going for an anaesthetic.

She simply could not understand why I didn't respond to her longing, especially when she was so terribly hungry. She rubbed herself against my legs time and again (this is her way of asking for food) with increasing fervour; when I didn't respond, she tried to climb up my dressing gown (something she has never done before or since) to tell me how badly she needed food. When that was no good, she sat down and mewed and mewed.

There was no way at all in which I could explain the situation to her; it was totally beyond her understanding. From her point of view, my response to her declared need was to take her, still without food she was sure was essential, to a place she finds frightening because she sees dogs there. (One of them howled, which made matters worse.) And we left her with strangers.

She forgave us in the evening, welcoming us in every way she could; but she didn't know what a lesson she had taught me. The analogy with human prayer to God which so often seems to go unanswered was so clear; the whole incident brought it home to me. And now Jess is fine and well and safely at home again. She is just as trusting, just as affectionate as ever, just as certain that we will provide for all her needs – and even more demanding of TLC. Perhaps that is another lesson.

ACKNOWLEDGEMENTS

My first acknowledgement goes to the cats themselves on parade in this book, but thanks are naturally also due to their patient owners who have taken the trouble to report on their pets and their antics.

It will be clear to those who read these pages that I have read many other writers' accounts of their cats. I am deeply indebted to them (living and dead) for their part in shaping my knowledge and understanding — especially my appreciation — of all that is embodied in the domestic cat.

Sources are made clear in the chapters themselves. If you are really into cats and have enjoyed this book, do increase your own appreciation of their great variety by extending your own reading. My library of cat books grows each year, while the monthly arrival of the UK's Your Cat magazine is always welcome. Wherever you live, support your cat charity: some such as the UK's Cats Protection publish worthy magazines themselves, though all are basically dedicated to re-homing unwanted cats and increasing owners' understanding.

Next my thanks go to my wife Sheila for her encouragement, not only in allowing me (and her) to be bossed by Skye and Arran but in helping improve the text, and to Anne and Lorna who have helped with research, typed the manuscript and made the index of named cats — not to mention allowing the cats to terrify (and intrigue) them in their office. It would be interesting to know if many look up cats with names such as Fuffino and Zambenflöte.

It has been fun working with my son Gareth as this book's originating publisher in Australia — especially since I pioneered the range of Southern Hemisphere titles imported into the UK. This has given the project an extra personal dimension. However, grateful though I am for his writing it, don't you think Gareth's piece about Sara at the end of Chapter 6 is based on exaggerated memory?

There is one other body of people to thank. It might sound a bit absurd, but thanks to everyone who has encouraged me to stop in the street to talk to their cat on the path or fence, or enjoyed my enjoying their cat on my lap, or just allowed me to be myself without restraint. Such people — nice, cat lovers — have played a useful part in my developing love of the species and my having been able to lead a successful life almost as crazy as that of the very cats themselves. Save us from those poor folk who can't see the point.

David St John Thomas

BIBLIOGRAPHY

Alderton, David, *Cats*, London, 1992

Anderson, Karen, *Why Cats Do That. A Collection of Curious Kitty Quirks*, Minocqua, 1958

Anderson, Niki, *What My Cat Has Taught Me About Life* - Meditations for Cat Lovers, Tulsa, 1997

Bessant, Claire, *What Cats Want*, London, 2002

-- *The Cat Whisperer. The Secret of how to Talk to Your Cat*, London, 2004

Byrne, Robert & Skelton, Teressa, *Quotable Cats. All the Best from the Literature of Cats*, London, 1985

Cats are Smarter than Jack, Ferntree Gully, Victoria, 2005

Cats Protection League (ed. Philip Wood), *A Passion for Cats*, Newton Abbot, 1987

Delderfield, Eric, *Eric Delderfield's Bumper Book of True Animal Stories*, Nairn, 1992

Evans, Mark, *The Complete Guide to Kitten Care*, London, 1996

Exley, Helen, *The Littlest Cat Book*, Watford & New York, 1999

Frazier, Anitra with Eckroate, Norma, *The Natural Cat*, New York, 1981

-- *It's A Cat's Life*, New York, 1985

Gallico, Paul, *The Silent Miaow. A Manual for Kittens, Strays and Homeless Cats*, New York, 1964

Gardiner, Andrew, *A-Z of Cat Health and First Aid. A holistic veterinary guide for owners*, London, 2002

Gay, John, *John Gay's Book of Cats*, Newton Abbot, 1975

Gilbert, John R., *Cats Cats Cats Cats*, London, 1961

Gooden, Mona, *The Poet's Life*, London, 1946

Haddon, Celia, *Cat Questions and Answers. A handbook of helpful and curious advice for cats and their owners*, London, 1999

-- *One Hundred Ways For a Cat to Train Its Human*, London, 2001

-- *One Hundred Secret Thoughts Cats Have About Humans*, London, 2001
-- *One Hundred Ways For a Cat to Find its Inner Kitten*, London, 2002
Heath, Sarah, *Why Does My Cat...?*, London, 1993
Henderson, G. N. & Coffey, D. J., *Cats and Cat Care. An International Encyclopedia*, Newton Abbot, 1973
Herriot, James, *James Herriot's Cat Stories*, London, 1994
Hudson, W. H., *Birds of Wing and other Wild Things*, London, 1930
-- *A Shepherd's Life*, London, 1936
Lauder, Phyllis, *The Rex Cat*, Newton Abbot, 1974
The Literary Cat, London, 1990
Loxton, *Caring for Your Cat*, Newton Abbot, 1975
McHattie, Grace, *That's Cats! A Compendium of Feline Facts*, Newton Abbot, 1991
Morris, Desmond, *Catlore*, London, 1987
National Trust, *A Treasury of Cat Tales & Trifles,* London, 2002
Necker, Claire, *The Natural History of Cats*, New York, 1977
Nown, Graham & Sylvana, *A Clowder of Cats*, London, 1989
O'Mara, Lesley (ed.), *Greatest Cat Stories*, London, 1995
O'Mara, Lesley, *Cats' Miscellany*, London, 2005
Quotable Cats. *The Quintessential Collections of Feline Wisdom*, London, 1997
Richter, Jack, *Your Talking Cat*, Chelmsford, undated
Rowse, A. L., *Three Cornish Cats*, London, 1974
-- *A Quartet of Cornish Cats*, Truro, 1986
Sayers, Susan, *Gospel for Cat Lovers*, Stowmarket, 2003
Surman, Richard, *The Times Book of Church Cats*, London, 1999
-- *Cathedral Cats*, London, 2005
Tangye, Derek, *A Cat in the Window*, London, 1962
-- *A Cat Affair*, London, 1974
Tylinek/Burger, *Big Book of Cats, The*, Newton Abbot, 1979

INDEX OF NAMED CATS

Also by David St John Thomas ...

JOURNEY THROUGH BRITAIN
Landscape, People and Books

For three years David St John Thomas travelled through Britain, exploring the fascinating and diverse character of Britain today. The result is a 700-page travelogue/commentary in the tradition of J. B. Priestley's *English Journey*.

From spending an evening with Patrick Moore or touring the Hebridean islands by ship, to travelling round the Lake District's coast by stopping train or savouring the continuing individuality of deepest Northumberland, the reader will quickly find the author a good companion and a reliable guide. David St John Thomas knows the nation well, both the familiar and the totally unexpected. He meets both famous and unknown people: old friends, authors, great gardeners, railwaymen, and many of those involved in the book business. Many seem to grow out of their landscape and all enrich the journey with their own stories and observations.

Journey through Britain is a rich and fertile collection of people, organisations, books, art galleries, crafts, cliffs and beaches, canals, county bus services, mountain moors, cruise ships and cycle ways. There are glimpses of Britain's industrial history, old seaside towns, early Christian sites, great hotels and restaurants, as well as its small islands, craft industries and rural revivals of many kinds. There is much to enjoy and celebrate but there is conflict, too, as the book occasionally pauses on the journey to recall human foibles and their consequences.

Sometimes erudite, constantly perceptive and always eye opening, this is a breezy and entertaining account of Britain as it really is.